FEAR**LESS**

PRAYER JOURNAL

This Journal belongs to

_____

FEARLESS

PERHAPS
THIS IS THE
Moment
FOR WHICH
YOU WERE
Created

TABLE OF CONTENTS

INTRODUCTION

WEAPONS FOR PRAYER

These pages contain fuel for your faith and ammunition from the Bible to live a life of victory and joy through prayer.

BOLD COURAGE PAGES

Boldly illustrated pages with Scripture to encourage your heart.

PERSONAL JOURNAL PAGES

God Speaks Today...

Man of God,

This journal is for you!

Never be ashamed of the ferocity and fervency of your love for God, and your belief in the power of the gospel.

When the Church of Jesus is filled with praying men, it is filled with strength.

Take these pages and let your heart bleed all over them as you intercede and press to take hold of all that God took hold of you for!

Your Prayer Journal is also packed with inspiring quotes on prayer, hundreds of Scriptures, as well as prayer resources such as the names of God, who you are in Christ, and many more tools for effective prayer and praise.

The FEARLESS Prayer Journal for Men of God is designed not just as a place to record, but to equip; an arsenal of Scripture and inspiration to feed your faith and set aflame your times of fellowship with the Father.

Consider these powerful words by E M Bounds, from his book, *Power Through Prayer*, a call that still rings true today, perhaps now more than ever...

> "What the Church needs today is not more machinery or better, not new organizations or more and novel methods, but men whom the Holy Ghost can use - men of prayer, men mighty in prayer. The Holy Ghost does not flow through methods, but through men. He does not come on machinery, but on men. He does not anoint plans, but men - **men of prayer**."

Be that man! You can render no greater service to your generation, and the last man standing will be the one who has taken time on his knees.

May strength and grace fill your spirit as you continue to step forward in faith.

ABOUT YOUR JOURNAL

10 great ways this journal will equip you for victory...

1. DATE...
The journal is not tied to any program. Each walk with God is personal, and our schedules and preferences are as unique as we are. Use it daily, weekly – whatever fits with your own spiritual journey with Jesus.

2. THANKYOU, LORD...
A place for answered prayers and appreciation of God's faithfulness!

3. THE WORD...
As a man of the Word the Holy Spirit will highlight Scriptures to you, the weapons of your warfare and wonderment. Make sure you never forget what He points out record them here!

4. INSPIRATION FOR YOUR PRAYER JOURNEY & GROWTH ...
Quotes from great men and women of God through the centuries, carefully chosen to fuel your own walk with Him today.

5. JOURNAL...
Plenty of room to record what you and your Papa in Heaven have been talking about.

6. PRAYER SCRIPTURES...
Encouragement from the Good Book to continue praying and never give up!

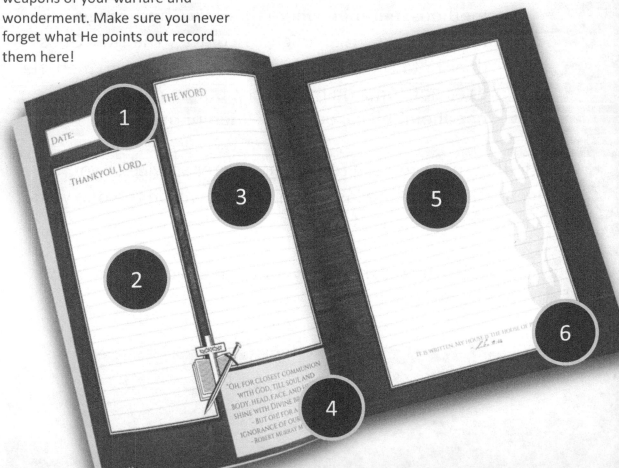

3

ALSO INCLUDED ...

7. OLD & NEW TESTAMENT IN 52 WEEKS
A 52 week plan to read through the entire Bible. Choose Old or New Testament or both and cover every word over a year. Tick each one as you complete it.

8. COURAGEOUS PAGES
Boldly designed inspirational pages to impart strength to your heart.

9. WEAPONS FOR PRAYER...
The Bible was designed as an arsenal for effective prayer and victorious living. Weapons For Prayer pages are potent resources for use in your times of prayer and praise.

10. ANSWERED PRAYER LOG
A diary of divine intervention where you can record your prayer answers and come back again and again to remember God's faithfulness.

BONUS RESOURCES

Throughout the journal you will also discover numerous extra resources prepared specifically to impact and inspire your deepening life of prayer and praise. All free and ready and waiting!

AND ALWAYS REMEMBER...

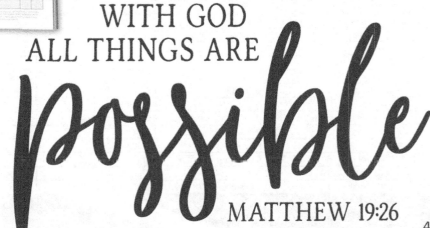

WITH GOD ALL THINGS ARE *possible*

MATTHEW 19:26

NEW TESTAMENT IN 52 WEEKS

Week	Monday	Tuesday	Wednesday	Thursday	Friday
1	☐ Mark 1	☐ Mark 2	☐ Mark 3	☐ Mark 4	☐ Mark 5
2	☐ Mark 6	☐ Mark 7	☐ Mark 8	☐ Mark 9	☐ Mark 10
3	☐ Mark 11	☐ Mark 12	☐ Mark 13	☐ Mark 14	☐ Mark 15
4	☐ Mark 16	☐ Acts 1	☐ Acts 2	☐ Acts 3	☐ Acts 4
5	☐ Acts 5	☐ Acts 6	☐ Acts 7	☐ Acts 8	☐ Acts 9
6	☐ Acts 10	☐ Acts 11	☐ Acts 12	☐ Acts 13	☐ Acts 14
7	☐ Acts 15	☐ Acts 16	☐ Acts 17	☐ Acts 18	☐ Acts 19
8	☐ Acts 20	☐ Acts 21	☐ Acts 22	☐ Acts 23	☐ Acts 24
9	☐ Acts 25	☐ Acts 26	☐ Acts 27	☐ Acts 28	☐ Hebrews 1
10	☐ Hebrews 2	☐ Hebrews 3	☐ Hebrews 4	☐ Hebrews 5	☐ Hebrews 6
11	☐ Hebrews 7	☐ Hebrews 8	☐ Hebrews 9	☐ Hebrews 10	☐ Hebrews 11
12	☐ Hebrews 12	☐ Hebrews 13	☐ Galatians 1	☐ Galatians 2	☐ Galatians 3
13	☐ Galatians 4	☐ Galatians 5	☐ Galatians 6	☐ James 1	☐ James 2
14	☐ James 3	☐ James 4	☐ James 5	☐ Matthew 1	☐ Matthew 2
15	☐ Matthew 3	☐ Matthew 4	☐ Matthew 5	☐ Matthew 6	☐ Matthew 7
16	☐ Matthew 8	☐ Matthew 9	☐ Matthew 10	☐ Matthew 11	☐ Matthew 12
17	☐ Matthew 13	☐ Matthew 14	☐ Matthew 15	☐ Matthew 16	☐ Matthew 17
18	☐ Matthew 18	☐ Matthew 19	☐ Matthew 20	☐ Matthew 21	☐ Matthew 22
19	☐ Matthew 23	☐ Matthew 24	☐ Matthew 25	☐ Matthew 26	☐ Matthew 27
20	☐ Matthew 28	☐ Romans 1	☐ Romans 2	☐ Romans 3	☐ Romans 4
21	☐ Romans 5	☐ Romans 6	☐ Romans 7	☐ Romans 8	☐ Romans 9
22	☐ Romans 10	☐ Romans 11	☐ Romans 12	☐ Romans 13	☐ Romans 14
23	☐ Romans 15	☐ Romans 16	☐ Ephesians 1	☐ Ephesians 2	☐ Ephesians 3
24	☐ Ephesians 4	☐ Ephesians 5	☐ Ephesians 6	☐ Philippians 1	☐ Philippians 2
25	☐ Philippians 3	☐ Philippians 4	☐ Colossians 1	☐ Colossians 2	☐ Colossians 3
26	☐ Colossians 4	☐ Philemon 1	☐ Luke 1	☐ Luke 2	☐ Luke 3
27	☐ Luke 4	☐ Luke 5	☐ Luke 6	☐ Luke 7	☐ Luke 8
28	☐ Luke 9	☐ Luke 10	☐ Luke 11	☐ Luke 12	☐ Luke 13
29	☐ Luke 14	☐ Luke 15	☐ Luke 16	☐ Luke 17	☐ Luke 18
30	☐ Luke 19	☐ Luke 20	☐ Luke 21	☐ Luke 22	☐ Luke 23
31	☐ Luke 24	☐ 1 Corinthians 1	☐ 1 Corinthians 2	☐ 1 Corinthians 3	☐ 1 Corinthians 4
32	☐ 1 Corinthians 5	☐ 1 Corinthians 6	☐ 1 Corinthians 7	☐ 1 Corinthians 8	☐ 1 Corinthians 9
33	☐ 1 Corinthians 10	☐ 1 Corinthians 11	☐ 1 Corinthians 12	☐ 1 Corinthians 13	☐ 1 Corinthians 14
34	☐ 1 Corinthians 15	☐ 1 Corinthians 16	☐ 2 Corinthians 1	☐ 2 Corinthians 2	☐ 2 Corinthians 3
35	☐ 2 Corinthians 4	☐ 2 Corinthians 5	☐ 2 Corinthians 6	☐ 2 Corinthians 7	☐ 2 Corinthians 8
36	☐ 2 Corinthians 9	☐ 2 Corinthians 10	☐ 2 Corinthians 11	☐ 2 Corinthians 12	☐ 2 Corinthians 13
37	☐ 1 Timothy 1	☐ 1 Timothy 2	☐ 1 Timothy 3	☐ 1 Timothy 4	☐ 1 Timothy 5
38	☐ 1 Timothy 6	☐ 2 Timothy 1	☐ 2 Timothy 2	☐ 2 Timothy 3	☐ 2 Timothy 4
39	☐ Titus 1	☐ Titus 2	☐ Titus 3	☐ 1 John 1	☐ 1 John 2
40	☐ 1 John 3	☐ 1 John 4	☐ 1 John 5	☐ 2 John 1	☐ 3 John 1
41	☐ 1 Peter 1	☐ 1 Peter 2	☐ 1 Peter 3	☐ 1 Peter 4	☐ 1 Peter 5
42	☐ John 1	☐ John 2	☐ John 3	☐ John 4	☐ John 5
43	☐ John 6	☐ John 7	☐ John 8	☐ John 9	☐ John 10
44	☐ John 11	☐ John 12	☐ John 13	☐ John 14	☐ John 15
45	☐ John 16	☐ John 17	☐ John 18	☐ John 19	☐ John 20
46	☐ John 21	☐ 1 Thessalonians 1	☐ 1 Thessalonians 2	☐ 1 Thessalonians 3	☐ 1 Thessalonians 4
47	☐ 1 Thessalonians 5	☐ 2 Thessalonians 1	☐ 2 Thessalonians 2	☐ 2 Thessalonians 3	☐ 2 Peter 1
48	☐ 2 Peter 2	☐ 2 Peter 3	☐ Jude 1	☐ Revelation 1	☐ Revelation 2
49	☐ Revelation 3	☐ Revelation 4	☐ Revelation 5	☐ Revelation 6	☐ Revelation 7
50	☐ Revelation 8	☐ Revelation 9	☐ Revelation 10	☐ Revelation 11	☐ Revelation 12
51	☐ Revelation 13	☐ Revelation 14	☐ Revelation 15	☐ Revelation 16	☐ Revelation 17
52	☐ Revelation 18	☐ Revelation 19	☐ Revelation 20	☐ Revelation 21	☐ Revelation 22

OLD TESTAMENT IN 52 WEEKS

Week	Monday	Tuesday	Wednesday	Thursday	Friday	Saturday
1	Gen 1-3	Gen 4-6	Gen 7-9	Gen 10-12	Gen 13-16	Gen 17-18
2	Gen 19-21	Gen 22-23	Gen 24	Gen 25-26	Gen 27-28	Gen 29-30
3	Gen 31-32	Gen 33-35	Gen 36-37	Gen 38-40	Gen 41	Gen 42-43
4	Gen 44-45	Gen 46-48	Gen 49 – Exo 1	Exo 2-4	Exo 5-7	Exo 8-9
5	Exo 10-12	Exo 13-15	Exo 16-18	Exo 19-21	Exo 22-24	Exo 25-26
6	Exo 27-28	Exo 29-30	Exo 31-33	Exo 34-35	Exo 36-37	Exo 38-39
7	Exo 40 – Lev 3	Lev 4-6	Lev 7-8	Lev 9-11	Lev 12-13	Lev 14-15
8	Lev 16-18	Lev 19-21	Lev 22-23	Lev 24-25	Lev 26-27	Num 1-2
9	Num 3	Num 4-5	Num 6	Num 7	Num 8-10	Num 11-13
10	Num 14-15	Num 16-17	Num 18-20	Num 21-22	Num 23-25	Num 26-27
11	Num 28-30	Num 31	Num 32	Num 33-34	Num 35-36	Deut 1-2
12	Deut 3-4	Deut 5-7	Deut 8-10	Deut 11-13	Deut 14-16	Deut 17-20
13	Deut 21-23	Deut 24-27	Deut 28	Deut 29-31	Deut 32-33	Deut 34 – Josh 3
14	Josh 4-6	Josh 7-9	Josh 10-12	Josh 13-14	Josh 15-16	Josh 17-18
15	Josh 19-20	Josh 21-22	Josh 23 – Judg 1	Judg 2-4	Judg 5-6	Judg 7-8
16	Judg 9-10	Judg 11-13	Judg 14-17	Judg 18-19	Judg 20-21	Ruth 1-4
17	1 Sam 1-3	1 Sam 4-7	1 Sam 8-10	1 Sam 11-13	1 Sam 14-15	1 Sam 16-17
18	1 Sam 18-19	1 Sam 20-22	1 Sam 23-24	1 Sam 25-27	1 Sam 28-31	2 Sam 1-2
19	2 Sam 3-5	2 Sam 6-9	2 Sam 10-12	2 Sam 13-14	2 Sam 15-17	2 Sam 18-19
20	2 Sam 20-21	2 Sam 22-23	2 Sam 24 – 1 Kin 1	1 Kin 2-3	1 Kin 4-6	1 Kin 7
21	1 Kin 8	1 Kin 9-10	1 Kin 11-12	1 Kin 13-14	1 Kin 15-16	1 Kin 17-19
22	1 Kin 20-21	1 Kin 22 – 2 Kin 1	2 Kin 2-3	2 Kin 4-5	2 Kin 6-8	2 Kin 9-10
23	2 Kin 11-13	2 Kin 14-16	2 Kin 17-18	2 Kin 19-21	2 King 22-24	2 Kin 25 – 1 Chr 1
24	1 Chr 2-3	1 Chr 4-5	1 Chr 6	1 Chr 7-8	1 Chr 9-10	1 Chr 11-12
25	1 Chr 13-15	1 Chr 16-18	1 Chr 19-22	1 Chr 23-24	1 Chr 25-26	1 Chr 27-29
26	2 Chr 1-4	2 Chr 5-7	2 Chr 8-11	2 Chr 12-16	2 Chr 17-19	2 Chr 20-23
27	2 Chr 24-26	2 Chr 27-29	2 Chr 30-32	2 Chr 33-35	2 Chr 36 – Ezra 1	Ezra 2-3
28	Ezra 4-7	Ezra 8-9	Ezra 10 – Neh 2	Neh 3-5	Neh 6	Neh 7
29	Neh 8-9	Neh 10-11	Neh 12-13	Esther 1-4	Esther 5-9	Esther 10 – Job 4
30	Job 5-7	Job 8-10	Job 11-13	Job 14-16	Job 17-19	Job 20-21
31	Job 22-25	Job 26-29	Job 30-31	Job 32-33	Job 34-36	Job 37-38
32	Job 39-41	Job 42 – Psa 6	Psa 7-13	Psa 14-17	Psa 18-22	Psa 23-28
33	Psa 29-33	Psa 34-36	Psa 37-39	Psa 40-45	Psa 46-50	Psa 51-56
34	Psa 57-63	Psa 64-68	Psa 69-72	Psa 73-76	Psa 77	Psa 78-79
35	Psa 80-84	Psa 85-88	Psa 89-91	Psa 92-97	Psa 98-103	Psa 104-105
36	Psa 106-107	Psa 108-113	Psa 114-118	Psa 119:1-88	Psa 119:89-176	Psa 120-130
37	Psa 131-136	Psa 137-143	Psa 144-148	Psa 149 – Prov 2	Prov 3-5	Prov 6-7
38	Prov 8-10	Prov 11-13	Prov 14-15	Prov 16-18	Prov 19-21	Prov 22-23
39	Prov 24-25	Prov 26-28	Prov 29-30	Prov 31 – Eccl 2	Eccl 3-6	Eccl 7-10
40	Eccl 11 – Song 4	Song 5 – Isa 1	Isa 2-5	Isa 6-9	Isa 10-13	Isa 14-18
41	Isa 19-22	Isa 23-26	Isa 27-29	Isa 30-33	Isa 34-37	Isa 38-40
42	Isa 41-43	Isa 44-47	Isa 48-51	Isa 52-56	Isa 57-60	Isa 61-65
43	Isa 66 – Jer 2	Jer 3-5	Jer 6-8	Jer 9-11	Jer 12-14	Jer 15-17
44	Jer 18-21	Jer 22-23	Jer 24-26	Jer 27-29	Jer 30-31	Jer 32-33
45	Jer 34-36	Jer 37-40	Jer 41-44	Jer 45-47	Jer 48	Jer 49-50
46	Jer 51	Jer 52 – Lam 2	Lam 3	Lam 4 – Ezek 1	Ezek 2-5	Ezek 6-9
47	Ezek 10-12	Ezek 13-15	Ezek 16	Ezek 17-19	Ezek 20-21	Ezek 22-23
48	Ezek 24-26	Ezek 27-29	Ezek 30-32	Ezek 33-35	Ezek 36-37	Ezek 38-39
49	Ezek 40-41	Ezek 42-44	Ezek 45-47	Ezek 48 – Dan 1	Dan 2-3	Dan 4-5
50	Dan 6-8	Dan 9-10	Dan 11 – Hos 1	Hos 2-6	Hos 7-11	Hos 12 – Joel 1
51	Joel 2 – Amos 1	Amos 2-5	Amos 6 – Obad 1	Jonah 1 – Micah 2	Micah 3-7	Nahum 1 – Hab 1
52	Hab 2 – Zeph 2	Zeph 3 – Zech 1	Zech 2-6	Zech 7-10	Zech 11-14	Mal 1-4

"ASLAN IS A LION- THE LION, THE GREAT LION." "OOH" SAID SUSAN. "I'D THOUGHT HE WAS A MAN. IS HE- QUITE SAFE? I SHALL FEEL RATHER NERVOUS ABOUT MEETING A LION"..."SAFE?" SAID MR BEAVER ..."WHO SAID ANYTHING ABOUT SAFE? 'COURSE HE ISN'T SAFE. BUT HE'S GOOD. HE'S THE KING, I TELL YOU."

— C.S. LEWIS, THE LION, THE WITCH AND THE WARDROBE

THE LION

OF THE TRIBE OF

JUDAH

THE ROOT OF DAVID, **HAS CONQUERED**

REVELATION 5.5

DATE:

THANKYOU, LORD...

THE WORD

> "TO AROUSE ONE MAN TO THE TREMENDOUS POWER OF PRAYER FOR OTHERS, IS WORTH MORE THAN THE COMBINED ACTIVITY OF A SCORE OF AVERAGE CHRISTIANS."
> - A. J. GORDON

HE THAT BELIEVETH ON ME, AS THE SCRIPTURE HATH SAID,
OUT OF HIS BELLY SHALL FLOW RIVERS OF LIVING WATER..

— John 7:38

DATE:

THANKYOU, LORD...

THE WORD

"DEPEND UPON IT, IF YOU ARE BENT ON PRAYER, THE DEVIL WILL NOT LEAVE YOU ALONE. HE WILL MOLEST YOU, TANTALIZE YOU, BLOCK YOU, AND WILL SURELY FIND SOME HINDRANCES, BIG OR LITTLE OR BOTH. AND WE SOMETIMES FAIL BECAUSE WE ARE IGNORANT OF HIS DEVICES DO NOT THINK HE MINDS OUR PRAYING ABOUT THINGS IF WE LEAVE IT AT THAT. WHAT HE MINDS, AND OPPOSES STEADILY, IS THE PRAYER THAT PRAYS ON UNTIL IT IS PRAYED THROUGH, ASSURED OF THE ANSWER."-- MARY BOOTH

I CALLED UPON THE LORD IN DISTRESS: THE LORD
ANSWERED ME, AND SET ME IN A LARGE PLACE.

- Psalms 118:5

DATE:

THANKYOU, LORD...

THE WORD

"OH, FOR CLOSEST COMMUNION WITH GOD, TILL SOUL AND BODY, HEAD, FACE, AND HEART - SHINE WITH DIVINE BRILLIANCY - BUT OH! FOR A HOLY IGNORANCE OF OUR SHINING!"
- ROBERT MURRAY M'CHEYNE

IT IS WRITTEN, MY HOUSE IS THE HOUSE OF PRAYER:
- *Luke 19:46*

DATE:

THANKYOU, LORD...

THE WORD

"DO NOT HAVE YOUR CONCERT FIRST, AND THEN TUNE YOUR INSTRUMENT AFTERWARDS. BEGIN THE DAY WITH THE WORD OF GOD AND PRAYER, AND GET FIRST OF ALL INTO HARMONY WITH HIM."
- JAMES HUDSON TAYLOR

THE RIGHTEOUS CRY, AND THE LORD HEARETH, AND
DELIVERETH THEM OUT OF ALL THEIR TROUBLES.

– Psalms 34:17

DATE:

THANKYOU, LORD...

THE WORD

"BEAR UP THE HANDS THAT HANG DOWN, BY FAITH AND PRAYER; SUPPORT THE TOTTERING KNEES. HAVE YOU ANY DAYS OF FASTING AND PRAYER? STORM THE THRONE OF GRACE AND PERSEVERE THEREIN, AND MERCY WILL COME DOWN."
- JOHN WESLEY

BUT WE WILL GIVE OURSELVES CONTINUALLY TO PRAYER,
AND TO THE MINISTRY OF THE WORD.

- Acts 6:4

NAMES & TITLES OF GOD

"EL" = TO BE STRONG, POWERFUL, OR MIGHTY.

Elohim The Creator God *Gen 1:1*
El Echad The One God *Malachi 1:1*
El Hanne'eman The Faithful God *Deut 7:9*
El Emet The God of Truth *Ps 31:5*
El-Beth-El The God of the House of God *Gen 3*
El Tsaddik The Righteous God *Isa 45:21*
El Shaddai The All Sufficient, Many Breasted *Gen 17:1*
El Elyon The Most High God *Gen 14:20; Ps 9:2*
El Olam The Everlasting God *Gen 21:33*
El Roi The God Who Sees Me *Gen 16:13-14*
El Gibbor The Mighty God *Isa 9:6*
El De'ot The God of Knowledge *1 Sam 2:3*
El Haggadol The Great God *Deut 10:17*
El Hakkavod The God of Glory *Ps 29:3*
El Hakkadosh The Holy God *Isa 5:16*
El Hashamayim The God of the Heavens *Ps 136:26*
El Chaiyai The God of my Life *Ps 42:8*
El Channum The Gracious God *Jonah 4:2*
El Rachum The God of Compassion and Mercy *Deut 4:31*
El Yeshuati The God of My Salvation *Isa 12:2*
El Yeshuatenu The God of Our salvation *Ps 68:19*
El-Kanna The Jealous God *Ex 20:5; Deut 4:24*
Elohim-Elyon God The Most High God *Ps 91:1-2*
El-Elohe-Israel God The God of Israel *Gen 33:20*
El Hannora The Awesome God *Neh 9:32*
Elohim T'Sabaoth Master, Ruler of All *Amos 4:13; Rom 9:29*
Immanu-el God Is With Us *Isa 7:14*

YHWH (LORD)

**The self existent One revealing Himself
to man in redemptive purpose.**

YHWH Elohim The Lord God Redeemer Creator. *Genesis 2:4*

YHWH Elohim Tseva'ot The Lord of Hosts *Ps 84:8, Jer 15:16*

YHWH Elohai The Lord My God *Psalm 13:3*

YHWH Osenu The Lord Our Maker *Psalm 95:6*

YHWH Jireh The Lord Who Sees ANd Provides *Gen 22:14*

YHWH Rapha The Lord Who Heals. *Ex 15:26*

YHWH Nissi The Lord my Banner. *Exodus 17:15*

YHWH Kanna The Lord who is jealous. *Exodus 20:5*

YHWH M'kaddesh The Lord who sanctifies. *Leviticus 20:8*

YHWH Shalom The Lord our Peace. *Judges 6:24*

YHWH Shaphat The Lord is judge. *Judges 11:27*

YHWH Elyon The Lord Most High. *Psalm 7:17*

YHWH Raah (Roi) The Lord my Shepherd. *Psalm 23:1*

YHWH Gibbor The Lord is Mighty. *Deut 10:17*

YHWH Tsidkenu The Lord our Righteousness *Jeremiah 23:6*

YHWH Sal'i The Lord My Rock *Psalm 18:2*

YHWH Tsuri v'goali The Lord My Rock & Redeemer *Psalm 19:14*

YHWH Shammah The Lord is there, ever present. *Ezekiel 48:35*

EACH REDEMPTIVE NAME REVEALS HOW GOD CAN MEET EVERY NEED OF MAN WITH HIS POWER.

NAMES RELATING TO GOD'S FATHERHOOD

My Father, and your Father *John 20:17*

Abba, Father (Daddy God) *Gal 4:6; Rom 8:15*

God our Father *1 Cor 1:3*

The Father of Mercies, The God of all Comfort *2 Cor 1:3*

one God, the Father, of whom are all things *1 Cor 8:6*

God the Father *Galatians 1:3*

the Father of glory *Ephesians 1:17*

Father of all, who is above all, and through all, and in you all *Eph 4:6*

the Father of spirits *Hebrews 12:9*

the Father of lights *James 1:17*

the God and Father of our Lord Jesus Christ *1 Peter 1:3*

God is Light and He is Love *1 John 1:5; 4:8*

DATE:

THANKYOU, LORD...

THE WORD

"THE MEN THAT WILL CHANGE THE COLLEGES AND SEMINARIES HERE REPRESENTED ARE THE MEN THAT WILL SPEND THE MOST TIME ALONE WITH GOD IT TAKES TIME FOR THE FIRES TO BURN. IT TAKES TIME FOR GOD TO DRAW NEAR AND FOR US TO KNOW THAT HE IS THERE. IT TAKES TIME TO ASSIMILATE HIS TRUTH. YOU ASK ME, HOW MUCH TIME? I DO NOT KNOW. I KNOW IT MEANS TIME ENOUGH TO FORGET TIME."
- JOHN R. MOTT

I WILL PRAY WITH THE SPIRIT, AND I WILL PRAY WITH THE UNDERSTANDING ALSO: I WILL SING WITH THE SPIRIT, AND I WILL SING WITH THE UNDERSTANDING ALSO.

– 1 Corinthians 14:15

DATE:

THANKYOU, LORD...

THE WORD

> "BEFORE THE GREAT REVIVAL IN GALLNEUKIRCHEN BROKE OUT, MARTIN BOOS SPENT HOURS AND DAYS AND OFTEN NIGHTS IN LONELY AGONIES OF INTERCESSION. AFTERWARDS, WHEN HE PREACHED, HIS WORDS WERE AS FLAME, AND THE HEARTS OF THE PEOPLE AS GRASS."
> - D.M. MCINTYRE

AND THEY CONTINUED STEADFASTLY IN THE APOSTLES
DOCTRINE AND FELLOWSHIP, AND IN BREAKING OF BREAD,
AND IN PRAYERS.
– Acts 2:42

DATE:

THANKYOU, LORD...

THE WORD

> "I HAVE SEEN MANY MEN WORK WITHOUT PRAYING, THOUGH I HAVE NEVER SEEN ANY GOOD COME OUT OF IT; BUT I HAVE NEVER SEEN A MAN PRAY WITHOUT WORKING."
> - JAMES HUDSON TAYLOR

IN MY DISTRESS I CALLED UPON THE LORD, AND CRIED
UNTO MY GOD: HE HEARD MY VOICE OUT OF HIS TEMPLE,
AND MY CRY CAME BEFORE HIM, EVEN INTO HIS EARS.

— Psalms 18:6

DATE:

THANKYOU, LORD...

THE WORD

"AH, PRAYER TURNS TREMBLING SAINTS INTO GREAT VICTORS! THERE IS NO SUCH THING AS SURRENDER, OR EVEN DISCOURAGEMENT, TO A MAN WHO DWELLS IN THE SECRET PLACE OF THE MOST HIGH AND ABIDES UNDER THE SHADOW OF THE ALMIGHTY."
-HENRY W. FROST

AND AS HE PRAYED, THE FASHION OF HIS COUNTENANCE
WAS ALTERED, AND HIS RAIMENT WAS WHITE AND
GLISTERING

— Luke 9:29

DATE:

THE WORD

THANKYOU, LORD...

"OH! MEN AND BRETHREN,
WHAT WOULD THIS HEART
FEEL IF I COULD BUT BELIEVE
THAT THERE WERE SOME
AMONG YOU WHO WOULD GO
HOME AND PRAY FOR A REVIVAL,
WHOSE FAITH IS LARGE ENOUGH,
AND THEIR LOVE FIERY ENOUGH
TO LEAD THEM FROM THIS
MOMENT TO EXERCISE
UNCEASING INTERCESSIONS THAT
GOD WOULD APPEAR AMONG US
AND DO WONDROUS THINGS
HERE, AS IN THE TIMES OF
FORMER GENERATIONS.."
-C. H. SPURGEON

29

BE CAREFUL FOR NOTHING; BUT IN EVERY THING BY
PRAYER AND SUPPLICATION WITH THANKSGIVING LET YOUR
REQUESTS BE MADE KNOWN UNTO GOD.
-Philippians 4:6

DATE:

THANKYOU, LORD...

THE WORD

"THE VALUE OF CONSISTENT
PRAYER IS NOT THAT HE
WILL HEAR US, BUT THAT
WE WILL HEAR HIM."
- WILLIAM MCGILL

REJOICE EVERMORE. PRAY WITHOUT CEASING. IN EVERY
THING GIVE THANKS: FOR THIS IS THE WILL OF GOD IN
CHRIST JESUS CONCERNING YOU.
– *1 Thessalonians 5:16–18*

DATE:

THANKYOU, LORD...

THE WORD

"WE CHRISTIANS TOO OFTEN SUBSTITUTE PRAYER FOR PLAYING THE GAME. PRAYER IS GOOD; BUT WHEN USED AS A SUBSTITUTE FOR OBEDIENCE, IT IS NOTHING BUT A BLATANT HYPOCRISY, A DESPICABLE PHARISAISM. TO YOUR KNEES, MAN! AND TO YOUR BIBLE! DECIDE AT ONCE! DON'T HEDGE! TIME FLIES! CEASE YOUR INSULTS TO GOD, QUIT CONSULTING FLESH AND BLOOD. STOP YOUR LAME, LYING, AND COWARDLY EXCUSES. ENLIST!."
- C. T. STUDD

HEAR ME WHEN I CALL, O GOD OF MY RIGHTEOUSNESS:
THOU HAST ENLARGED ME WHEN I WAS IN DISTRESS; HAVE
MERCY UPON ME, AND HEAR MY PRAYER.

Psalms 4:1

DATE:

THANKYOU, LORD...

THE WORD

"THE REASON WHY MANY FAIL
IN BATTLE IS BECAUSE THEY
WAIT UNTIL THE HOUR OF
BATTLE. THE REASON WHY
OTHERS SUCCEED IS BECAUSE
THEY HAVE GAINED THEIR
VICTORY ON THEIR KNEES LONG
BEFORE THE BATTLE CAME.
ANTICIPATE YOUR BATTLES;
FIGHT THEM ON YOUR KNEES
BEFORE TEMPTATION COMES,
AND YOU WILL ALWAYS HAVE
VICTORY." - R. A. TORREY

AND ALL THINGS, WHATSOEVER YE SHALL ASK IN PRAYER,
BELIEVING, YE SHALL RECEIVE.
- Matthew 21:22

FEEDING ON HEAVEN'S MANNA

Feed the spiritual side of your life. Read good books that expand your vision of what is possible. Watch videos and TV that will edify, encourage and fuel the fire of God burning in your heart. Ungodly literature and conversation are like water on the fire. Wholesome and Godly counsel is like gasoline!

Paul says in Galatians 6:8;
"For he who sows to his flesh will of the flesh reap corruption, but he who sows to the Spirit will of the Spirit reap everlasting life."

I have noticed that if I neglect Bible reading and prayer (sowing to the Spirit) and watch too much TV or too many movies (sowing to the flesh) it corrupts my life with God. It corrupts my hunger for the things of God and the move of God. However, during seasons of prayer, fasting and study, not only is my hunger satisfied, it is intensified. The more I get the more I want. The more I seek, the more I find, the more I am provoked to seek even further.

God's rich and wonderful undeserved graces are unfathomable.

READING IS FEEDING

One of the most effective ways to develop a hungry passion for God is to read. I was never much of a reader in my youth, but from about age 16 on, I began to develop a real love for the written word. It is here that I feed the fire in my spirit with life-giving fuel.

Jesus said in John 6:63:
"It is the Spirit who gives life; the flesh profits nothing. The words that I speak to you are spirit, and they are life."

Words are powerful. They are like containers that when opened spill their contents into the soul and imagination.
If you read books about great men and women, and moves of God, it develops a thirst in your soul to see the same. Often our imaginations are restricted by the limited experience of God in our own lives and congregations. Undoubtedly, many of these things will be good and significant, however, it is essential that we stretch the tent pegs of our mind and embrace the possibility of more. One way to do this is by feeding your spirit with stories of past moves of God, and allowing your heart to project those visions onto your own community and nation.

Get hold of some books about the Lewis revival in Scotland under Duncan Campbell. Read some of Charles Finney's own accounts of the revivals that he was involved in. Study the awesome ministry of the Booth's and the Salvation Army in their heyday. One of the most moving for are are the accounts of the Fulton Street Prayer Revival in 1857.

Friend, these accounts cannot fail but stir a hunger to see again the things that others have experienced. Fill your library with books by tried and tested God chasers; A W Tozer, Kathryn Kuhlman, Andrew Murray, E M Bounds, Oswald J Smith, Watchman Nee, to name just a few. Allow the experiences of others to propel you onward toward God's zealous purpose for your life and ministry.

Don't settle for what you know to be less than God's best. Build pictures of possibility on the inside and pray them into manifestation.

If books are not your thing, listen to audio or watch video. Check out sermonindex.net for hundreds of free audio sermons by revivalists with present and past. One way or another, it is essential that you feed your spiritual life with edifying material and fire baptized words.

Ensure that you give precedence to the scriptures themselves. Take time to read and meditate in the Word of God. Look into the life of Jesus. Glean from the accounts of others who have gone before. Learn methods of study and become a student of God's Word, building it systematically into your life. Ask God each time you read to help you understand it, and allow the Holy Spirit to enlighten your mind. Most importantly of all, act upon what He shows you.
I am always amazed, and somewhat dismayed, at how few Christians ever undertake a thorough study of the Scriptures in a systematic way. The Biblical illiteracy that is present in many of our churches is shocking.

God has provided all we need, but how many fail to avail themselves of the promises simply because they do not even know what they are!

Of all the recommendations I can offer you with regard to developing a root of righteousness and an unquenchable longing for God it would be this - fall in love with the Scriptures.

The words of the Bible are supernatural. They change a man or a woman from the inside out.
There are numerous avenues to accomplish this, and they do not necessarily require that you attend a college or make radical decisions that affect what you are already doing in your life. One way would be to sign up for the school that I developed. It is a complete and thorough study of all the major doctrines and books of the Bible, in an easy to access online school that you consume at your own pace and to fit with your necessary schedule.

Listen to heart-stirring teaching and preaching as you travel or cook or workout at the gym. Look for such already existing places in your schedule that provide windows of possibility to feed your spirit. It make take some choices and some creativity, but no one is in a position where they cannot invite more of God's word into their every day.

Make the decision to invest in your spiritual growth in the same way that you invest to develop your professional, educational and social life. All of us pour finance, time, thought ad energy into these aspects of our life.

How much more important is your spiritual growth than the natural? Yet our time and money flies in every other direction.

I say, enough with my excuses! Enough with my pandering! I love this amazing from Paul's admonition to Timothy:

"For physical training is of some value (useful for a little), but godliness (spiritual training) is useful and of value in everything and in every way, for it holds promise for the present life and also for the life which is to come."
1 Timothy 4:8 AMPLIFIED

Investment in your spiritual growth and maturity reaps eternal results, but the seeds of those results are sown little-by-little on a daily basis. I apply the same principle in my physical exercise regime, and have found that little and often yields excellent and marked results.

Too many well-meaning believers are waiting for a cataclysmic change to hit their busy schedule before they spend time with God. It is easy to deceive yourself into thinking that if you don't spend several hours then it is not worth spending any time. If 5 minutes is all you have, give those 5 to seek Him. If your hour-long drive to work is usually spent on frivolous radio shows turn your dashboard into an altar and use the time for prayer.

Look for opportunities that already exist and harness them. Beyond that begin to be intentional. Set aside specific time to seek and pray. Build a life of prayer, rather than just appending a few hurried prayers to your over-active calendar.

Don't waste another day waiting for some titanic revelation to rock your world - take a simple, manageable step this day, and every day that follows, and you will see tangible growth and breakthrough faster than you might expect.

The Spirit Life Bible School could provide the spiritual nutrition required for the next stages in your journey for many months and even years to come.

The school is available for free at **StudytheBibleNow**.com

* * *

Notes & References Relevant to what you have just been reading: Galatians 6:8; John 6:63; Isaiah 54:2; 2 Timothy 2:15; Ephesians 1:17-20; Romans 15:4; Proverbs 2:1-6; John 16:13; 1 John 2:27; James 1:25

Excerpt from Discovering & Developing a Passion For God by David Lee Martin

DATE:

THANKYOU, LORD...

THE WORD

"THE REASON WHY WE
OBTAIN NO MORE IN PRAYER
IS BECAUSE WE EXPECT NO
MORE. GOD USUALLY
ANSWERS US ACCORDING TO
OUR OWN HEARTS."
-RICHARD ALLELNE

AND THE LORD, HE IT IS THAT DOTH GO BEFORE THEE; HE
WILL BE WITH THEE, HE WILL NOT FAIL THEE, NEITHER
FORSAKE THEE: FEAR NOT, NEITHER BE DISMAYED.

– Deuteronomy 31:8

DATE:

THANKYOU, LORD...

THE WORD

"A PRAYERLESS MAN IS PROUD AND INDEPENDENT, AND ANY CHURCH THAT NEGLECTS CORPORATE PRAYER IS SADLY NO BETTER. ONLY GOD'S HUMBLE AND NEEDY CHILDREN TAKE THE TIME TO PRAY. EVERYONE ELSE IS JUST GOING THROUGH THE MOTIONS AND NAIVELY TRUSTING IN THEIR OWN STRENGTH."
-DAVID SMITHERS

AND WHEN HE WAS AT THE PLACE, HE SAID UNTO THEM,
PRAY THAT YE ENTER NOT INTO TEMPTATION.
— *Luke 22:40*

DATE:

THANKYOU, LORD...

THE WORD

"HE CAN DO ALL THINGS
WHO PRAYS WELL. ALL SOUL-
WINNERS HAVE CONQUERED
ON THEIR KNEES. WHEREVER
THE SECRET OF PREVAILING
PRAYER IS FOUND,
SOMETHING SUPERNATURAL
WILL COME TO PASS."
-G. F. OLIVER

CONFESS YOUR FAULTS ONE TO ANOTHER, AND PRAY ONE
FOR ANOTHER, THAT YE MAY BE HEALED. THE EFFECTUAL
FERVENT PRAYER OF A RIGHTEOUS MAN AVAILETH MUCH.-

- James 5:16

DATE:

THANKYOU, LORD...

THE WORD

"A SERMON IN SHOES IS
OFTEN MORE ELOQUENT
THAN A SERMON ON PAPER."
-THEODORE L. CUYLER

FOR GOD IS MY WITNESS, WHOM I SERVE WITH MY SPIRIT IN
THE GOSPEL OF HIS SON, THAT WITHOUT CEASING I MAKE
MENTION OF YOU ALWAYS IN MY PRAYERS.

- Romans 1:9

Tabernacle Prayer

"THERE I WILL MEET WITH YOU AND, FROM ABOVE THE MERCY SEAT, FROM BETWEEN THE TWO CHERUBIM THAT ARE UPON THE ARK OF THE TESTIMONY, I WILL SPEAK INTIMATELY WITH YOU..."

Exodus 25:22

A NEW & LIVING WAY

God revealed in the Tabernacle of Moses a way to approach Him. The form of things in the Old Testament often shadow what the New Testament gives substance to, and the natural things commanded by God reflect spiritual realities that come to completion in Jesus Christ *(Colossians 2:17)*.

Just as a shadow indicates the existence of the object caught in the light, so the natural things in scripture often indicate and reflect the existence of something of enduring substance and reality in the spiritual realm. The shadow is not the real thing, it merely points to it. So it is with the Tabernacle of Moses.

We need to understand that we are not talking about a mere method of praying here, but an actual place in heaven, into which God has invited us! We find in the Book of Hebrews that the earthly tabernacle was simply a copy (or a shadow) of the true spiritual tabernacle which exists in Heaven.

*"**who serve the copy and shadow of the heavenly things**, as Moses was divinely instructed when he was about to make the tabernacle. For He said, "See that you make all things according to the pattern shown you on the mountain.""* Hebrews 8:5

It is in this Heavenly Tabernacle that the Father sits in royal authority over the universe, and here that Jesus Christ ministers today.

*"Now this is the main point of the things we are saying: We have such a High Priest, who is seated at the right hand of the throne of the Majesty in the heavens, **a Minister of the sanctuary** and of the true tabernacle which the Lord erected, and not man."* Hebrews 8:1-2
"But Christ came as High Priest of the good things to come, with the greater and more perfect tabernacle not made with hands, that is, not of this creation." Hebrews 9:11

APPROACHING GOD

The Old Testament Tabernacle reveals a prescribed way to approach the Father in faith and holiness. In their ministry to God the priests under the Old Covenant followed clearly defined steps, which ensured that when they stood in the presence of the Lord, He would receive them and answer their requests.

Under the New Covenant, every believer is a priest *(1 Peter 2:9)*. Of course, we can approach God freely as our Father at any time, without fear of reproach or condemnation. The mode of approach foreshadowed in the earthly Tabernacle, however, reveals to us a consecrated way of entering boldly into the presence of God, one which is well pleasing to Him. Because of this, a great grace and empowerment comes upon anyone who chooses to come to God in this way.

*"Therefore, brethren, having boldness to enter the Holiest by the blood of Jesus, **by a new and living way which He consecrated for us**, through the veil, that is, His flesh, and having a High Priest over the house of God, let us draw near with a true heart in full assurance of faith, having our hearts sprinkled from an evil conscience and our bodies washed with pure water."* Hebrews 10:19-22

I encourage you to persist and ask God to reveal these things to you, that you may enjoy this heavenly privilege of access. As sure as the Word is true, as we behold Him in all His wondrous aspects, we will be changed into the very same image (2 Cor 3:18).

Throughout your journey through the Tabernacle mix both fellowship and intercessory prayer.

Do not think that you must go through the 'gauntlet' of each stage before you present your petitions and requests to God. His ear is open to the prayer of the righteous at any moment.

From 'Tabernacle Prayer – An Interactive Guide' by David Lee Martin, available free at JesusChrist.co.uk/tabernacle-prayer

Praying Through The Tabernacle....

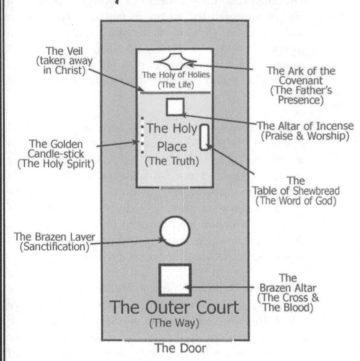

The Veil
(taken away
in Christ)

The Holy of Holies
(The Life)

The Ark of the
Covenant
(The Father's
Presence)

The Holy
Place
(The Truth)

The Altar of Incense
(Praise & Worship)

The Golden
Candle-stick
(The Holy Spirit)

The
Table of Shewbread
(The Word of God)

The Brazen Laver
(Sanctification)

The
Brazen Altar
(The Cross &
The Blood)

The Outer Court
(The Way)

The Door

THE BRAZEN ALTAR

Every day you must come to the cross of Jesus Christ. There you worship the Lord. There you see God judging your sin through Jesus Christ and step from the old to the new.

1. Say:
"Dear Jesus Christ. I worship You for Your blood. I thank You because Your blood forgave all of my sins. All of the sins that I have committed, and all of the sins which I am going to commit in the future, You have forgiven eternally."

2. Pray this prayer:
"Jesus, I worship You because through the blood You have delivered me from the power of Satan and the world. You move me to the Kingdom of Jesus Christ. Now I am living in Your Son's Kingdom through the blood of Jesus Christ."

3. Pray:
"I praise You for the blood of Jesus Christ because that blood declares to me that I was completely freed from all kinds of sickness and infirmity. Jesus, through the stripes which You received at the courtyard of Pilate, my sickness and diseases have been taken away since 2,000 years ago. I praise You for divine healing through the blood of Jesus Christ."

4. Pray:
"Dear Jesus, through Your blood I have been redeemed from the Adamic curse. Because of Adam the earth was cursed. The earth was to bring forth thistles and thorns. That is the symbol of all the failure in life. Oh God, You took our curse on the cross. Because the Bible says that Christ has redeemed us from the curse of the law becoming a curse for us that the blessing of Abraham might come upon the Gentiles. So through Your blood I am completely delivered from the curse. I am delivered from failure and poverty. I am free from the curse. I have the blessings of Abraham. I am a blessed person."

5. Next, pray:
"Dear Jesus, through Your blood I am delivered from death and hell. Jesus, You died and You were resurrected. You conquered death and hell. You brought the glory of the Kingdom of heaven. By the blood of Jesus Christ I am completely delivered from death and hell and am now living in the glory of Jesus Christ. I am a member of the kingdom of God. I have the eternal Kingdom in me so I praise God because of the blood. I worship Jesus and praise Him because of the blood."

THE BRAZEN LAVER - PLACE OF SANCTIFICATION

In the courtyard you move from the brazen altar to the laver. The laver is full of water. Before the high priest entered the Holy place, he washed his hands and feet. He was cleansed and sanctified. This is a picture of the Word of God and the Spirit of God Who change and sanctifies us.

1. Pray:
"Oh God, make me righteous through Your grace. Heavenly Father, make me truthful. Please help me not to live in lies. Let me not tell lies. Let me he a truthful person before You and before othcr people. "

2. Then pray:
"Heavenly Father, make me a faithful person. Loyal to God. Make me very faithful and loyal to God."

3. Pray:
"Oh God, let me not break God's Law, so that I will be loved by You. Make me very faithful and loyal, especially as far as the Ten Commandments are concerned."
Take time to meditate and search your heart in the light of the ten commandments and other portions of the Word of God that the Holy Spirit brings to your remembrance (Exodus 20).

4. Then pray for personal sanctification:
"Father, make me holy and sanctified. make me a holy person. Cleanse my heart so that it is pure."

5. Pray:
"Father, give me grace to forgive and love. make me a gentle and loving person. Make me an understanding and kind person."

6. Pray:
"Father, make me a very humble and meek person. Give me a soft heart toward people."

7. Then Pray:
"Oh God, help me to live according to the measure of faith that You gave me. Don 't make me proud. Make me live according to the faith of Jesus Christ that resides in my spirit."

THE HOLY PLACE

THE GOLDEN CANDLESTICK - THE HOLY SPIRIT

The Golden Candlestick represents the Holy Spirit. Here we throw ourselves in dependency upon Him.

1. Pray:
"Dear Holy Spirit, I recognize You. I welcome You. I adore You. Thank You for being in my life. You are my Senior Partner. You are the Spirit of God, and the Spirit of Jesus Christ. You are the Spirit of wisdom. You are the Spirit of understanding. You are the Spirit of counsel. You are the Spirit of power. You are the Spirit of the revelation of the Word of God. You are the Spirit of reverence which gives me thc power to reveal God. So help me now. I cannot do anything without Your anointing. I depend upon You. I worship You. I thank You."

THE TABLE OF SHEWBREAD - THE WORD OF GOD - JESUS CHRIST

1. Pray, "Lord, I delight in the Word of God. I admire and love the Word of God. I long after the Word of God. I read, I study, I believe, I act, I thank You, and I want to teach this Word of God. So, Lord give me a new fresh revelation in my heart. My heart is pantng for the Word of God. Please give me fresh revelation each day to live by."

2. Acknowledge Christ as the Living Word. Pray that you will hear His voice as your Shepherd. Honor and love Him. Dedicate your self to follow Him.

INCENSE ALTAR - PRAISE AND WORSHIP

The incense on this altar is praise and prayer to the Heavenly Father.

1. Come to this place and pray:
"I really appreciate You. You delivered me from sin. You delivered me from worldliness. You delivered me from sickness. You delivered me from the curse. You delivered me from death. You are the God who is the foundation of my life. You are the purpose of my life. You are the value of my life. I worship You, the God who created thc heaven and the earth and all things in them. I worship You. I thank You."

2. Sing praises to the Lord, then begin to speak from your heart for a long time.

THE HOLY OF HOLIES

ARK OF THE COVENANT - THE HOLY OF HOLIES - THE PRESENCE OF THE FATHER

When you come to the Holy of Holies and see the blood on the ark of the covenant, you are in the presence of God, right in front of the throne of God.

1. Pray, "I am eternally forgiven. I am eternally declared righteous. I am eternally saved. I am eternally blessed by His blood covenant. I thank You, dear Heavenly Father. I am now a member of Your Family. I am Your child and I joy in the triune God. I am living in the Holy of Holies. Abba, Father, I have many requests. I want You to hear them and help me. "

2. Pray all the things you want to receive from the Lord and thank Him for them.

3. Spend as much time as you are able or want to here before the Father, fellowshipping with Him, loving and listening.

2. Sing praises to the Lord, and continue praying in tongues and your known language until you are fully satisfied.

I CAN DO **ALL THINGS** THROUGH HIM WHO STRENGTHENS ME

PHILIPPIANS 4:13

DATE:

THANKYOU, LORD...

THE WORD

"ARE YOU LIVING FOR
THE THINGS YOU ARE
PRAYING FOR?."
-AUSTIN PHELPS

REJOICING IN HOPE; PATIENT IN TRIBULATION;
CONTINUING INSTANT IN PRAYER.
— *Romans 12:12*

DATE:

THANKYOU, LORD...

THE WORD

"THE TIME FACTOR IN PRAYER IS VERY IMPORTANT. IN THE EXERCISE OF PRAYER GOD IS NOT TIED TO OUR CLOCKS. NEITHER IS HE AT THE OTHER END OF THE PHONE TO RECEIVE AND ANSWER OUR TWO-MINUTE CALLS. IT TAKES TIME TO KNOW THE MIND OF GOD, TO SHUT OUT THE MATERIAL THINGS OF EARTH AND TO BE WHOLLY ABANDONED."
-HUGH C. C. MCCULLOUGH

AND BEING IN AN AGONY HE PRAYED MORE EARNESTLY:
AND HIS SWEAT WAS AS IT WERE GREAT DROPS OF BLOOD
FALLING DOWN TO THE GROUND.
— *Luke 22:44*

DATE:

THE WORD

THANKYOU, LORD...

"WE NEED A BAPTISM OF CLEAR
SEEING. WE DESPERATELY NEED
SEERS WHO CAN SEE THROUGH
THE MIST - CHRISTIAN LEADERS
WITH PROPHETIC VISION. UNLESS
THEY COME SOON IT WILL BE
TOO LATE FOR THIS GENERATION.
AND IF THEY DO COME WE WILL
NO DOUBT CRUCIFY A FEW OF
THEM IN THE NAME OF OUR
WORLDLY ORTHODOXY."
-A. W. TOZER

AND WHATSOEVER YE SHALL ASK IN MY NAME, THAT WILL I
DO, THAT THE FATHER MAY BE GLORIFIED IN THE SON.

- John 14:13

DATE:

THANKYOU, LORD...

THE WORD

"WE MUST CONTINUE IN
PRAYER IF WE ARE TO GET AN
OUTPOURING OF THE SPIRIT.
CHRIST SAYS THERE ARE SOME
THINGS WE SHALL NOT GET,
UNLESS WE PRAY AND FAST, YES,
"PRAYER AND FASTING. WE MUST
CONTROL THE FLESH AND
ABSTAIN FROM WHATEVER
HINDERS DIRECT FELLOWSHIP
WITH GOD."
- ANDREW BONAR

COMMIT THY WORKS UNTO THE LORD,
AND THY THOUGHTS SHALL BE ESTABLISHED.

— Proverbs 16:3

DATE:

THANKYOU, LORD...

THE WORD

"I WOULD RATHER TRAIN
TWENTY MEN TO PRAY, THAN
A THOUSAND TO PREACH; -
A MINISTER'S HIGHEST
MISSION OUGHT TO BE TO
TEACH HIS PEOPLE TO PRAY."
-H. MACGREGOR

THESE ALL CONTINUED WITH ONE ACCORD IN PRAYER AND
SUPPLICATION, WITH THE WOMEN, AND MARY THE MOTHER
OF JESUS, AND WITH HIS BRETHREN.
– *Acts 1:14*

DATE:

THANKYOU, LORD...

THE WORD

"WHEREVER THE CHURCH IS
AROUSED AND THE WORLD'S
WICKEDNESS ARRESTED,
SOMEBODY HAS BEEN PRAYING"
-A. T. PIERSON

MY VOICE SHALT THOU HEAR IN THE MORNING, O LORD;
IN THE MORNING WILL I DIRECT MY PRAYER UNTO THEE,
AND WILL LOOK UP.
– Psalms 5:3

THE WORD

THANKYOU, LORD...

"THE MISSIONARY CHURCH IS A PRAYING CHURCH. THE HISTORY OF MISSIONS IS A HISTORY OF PRAYER. EVERYTHING VITAL TO THE SUCCESS OF THE WORLD'S EVANGELIZATION HINGES ON PRAYER. ARE THOUSANDS OF MISSIONARIES AND TENS OF THOUSANDS OF NATIVE WORKERS NEEDED? PRAY YE THEREFORE THE LORD OF THE HARVEST, THAT HE SEND FORTH LABORERS INTO HIS HARVEST."
-JOHN R. MOTT

AND WE KNOW THAT ALL THINGS WORK TOGETHER FOR
GOOD TO THEM THAT LOVE GOD, TO THEM WHO ARE THE
CALLED ACCORDING TO HIS PURPOSE.

– Romans 8:28

DATE:

THANKYOU, LORD...

THE WORD

"NO SYSTEM OF DOCTRINE, PREACHING AND WORSHIP WHICH FAILS TO DEVELOP PRAYER, FAITH, SPIRITUAL LABOR, AND SUCCESS IN CONVERTING SOULS FROM SIN, CAN LONG HAVE THE FACE TO CLAIM TO BE THE RELIGION OF JESUS CHRIST!"
-WILLIAM W. PATTON

IF ANY OF YOU LACK WISDOM, LET HIM ASK OF GOD, THAT
GIVETH TO ALL MEN LIBERALLY, AND UPBRAIDETH NOT;
AND IT SHALL BE GIVEN HIM.

– James 1:5

DATE:

THANKYOU, LORD...

THE WORD

"HOW TERRIBLE IS THE COST OF ROBBING GOD OF TIME FOR PRAYER. WHEN WE ROB GOD OF TIME FOR QUIET, WE ARE ROBBING HIM OF OURSELVES. IT IS ONLY IN THE QUIET THAT WE CAN REALLY KNOW HIM AND KNOW OURSELVES, AND BE SURE THAT WE GIVE OURSELVES BACK TO HIM. OH, FOR GOD'S SAKE, DO NOT RISK KEEPING THE WINDOWS OF HEAVEN CLOSED BY ROBBING GOD OF TIME."
-GORDON M. GUINNESS

PRAY WITHOUT CEASING
- 1 Thessalonians 5:17

DATE:

THANKYOU, LORD...

THE WORD

"THIS MUCH IS SURE IN ALL
CHURCHES, FORGETTING PARTY
LABELS; THE SMALLEST MEETING
NUMERICALLY IS THE PRAYER-
MEETING. IF WEAK IN PRAYER WE
ARE WEAK EVERYWHERE."
-LEONARD RAVENHILL

BUT WITHOUT FAITH IT IS IMPOSSIBLE TO PLEASE HIM: FOR HE
THAT COMETH TO GOD MUST BELIEVE THAT HE IS, AND THAT
HE IS A REWARDED OF THEM THAT DILIGENTLY SEEK HIM.

— Hebrews 11:6

DATE:

THANKYOU, LORD...

THE WORD

"THE HISTORY OF MISSIONS IS THE HISTORY OF ANSWERED PRAYER. FROM PENTECOST TO THE HAYSTACK MEETING IN NEW ENGLAND AND FROM THE DAYS WHEN ROBERT MORRISON LANDED IN CHINA TO THE MARTYRDOM OF JOHN AND BETTY STAM, PRAYER HAS BEEN THE SOURCE OF POWER AND THE SECRET OF SPIRITUAL TRIUMPH."
- SAMUEL ZWEMER

ASK, AND IT SHALL BE GIVEN YOU; SEEK, AND YE SHALL
FIND; KNOCK, AND IT SHALL BE OPENED UNTO YOU.
– Matthew 7:7

DIALOGUE WITH GOD

"Prayer is not monologue, but dialogue; God's voice is its most essential part. Listening to God's voice is the secret of the assurance that He will listen to mine."
— *Andrew Murray*

Prayer is not meant to be a monologue, where we throw a multitude of words heavenward, say amen and leave the room.

God wants to speak to us on all occasions, and has made provision for us to be able to hear him in lots of different ways.

This richness of dynamic dialogue with God is what makes prayer so exciting. Throughout the Bible we read of men and women who entered into a conversational intimacy with the Father, and that same privilege is open to us.

God speaks in many ways including but not limited to dreams and visions, through the written or spoken Word, or in the still small voice on the inside of your heart. It could be an audible voice, although I think that is rare. More often God will speak in ways that require us to listen carefully and intentionally. He is interested in relationship and relationships are developed most strongly when we grow ever more sensitive to one another's voice and communication.

Hearing God is a whole other book, but as I said earlier, we learn to pray by praying. It may sound simplistic, but we learn to hear by listening.

I love the words that the Holy Spirit inspired in this regard:

"Incline your ear…" Proverbs 4:20 NKJV

Lean in to listen.

Still the other noise of life that hounds for your attention and crave his whispers.

When you do this you will surely begin to sense what He is saying to you. Clarity comes as we hone our ear to perceive what God is speaking, and then don't discount what we hear.

A big problem I have noticed with people is that they do hear Him, but immediately brush off what they hear as their own thoughts. They see a picture and ascribe it to the pizza they ate the night before.

Of course, we do get it wrong sometimes, or we misunderstand or misinterpret, but that should not be our default position or expectancy. As children of God it is natural for us to receive from Him. Our eyes and ears have been opened to perceive the spiritual world, and especially His voice.

"My sheep hear my voice…" John 10:27 KJV

This is the place we begin. By faith.

"I am His sheep. I hear His voice!"

That should be your absolute expectation. Know also that hearing God, and interpreting what you hear with clarity, is something that you can develop and improve at. How do we improve? We do it! We practice it.

Begin by asking questions.

"What do you have to say to me today, Lord?"

"How do you see me, Lord?"

"What would you like to say to this person to encourage them?"

Start with simple questions and listen for the answer. Yes/No questions are always worth practicing with. As you grow in confidence the dialogue expands and the conversation deepens.

Don't ever settle for one way traffic in prayer. Real excitement and adventure arise from conversing with Heaven and seeing His words go to work in your life. Just as Jesus described His mode of operation as not doing or saying anything that He had not already seen or heard His Father doing, so it can be for you and I.

"I speak that which I have seen with my Father" John 8:38 KJV

One of my favorite ways to dialogue, and to be brutally honest one I avoided for years (to my own regret) is through what some call two-way journaling. This concept of journaling is so much more than keeping a spiritual diary. It is a means of ongoing conversation. Mark Virkler's book, *4 Keys To Hearing God's Voice*, impacted my life significantly in this regard.

Essentially the four keys he encourages everyone to practice are very simple:

1. **Still your heart and mind** before God.

2. **Look for vision**, looking to Jesus, letting God use the faculty of your imagination to show you pictures.

3. **Listen for spontaneous thoughts** bubbling up from your spirit - be open to God interjecting and don't dismiss what you hear.

4. **Journal your conversations** - write down your thoughts, prayers and questions, but don't stop there. Scribe God's responses.

When I began doing this, first writing down my question, and then by faith writing His answer, freely and spontaneously not second-guessing myself, I was literally swept away at what began to happen. Among other things, God spoke to me about the exact time I would move home, specific words for friends and family, incredible insights about my own soul and my calling to write, and so much more. He navigated me through some of the toughest most insecure times I have ever experienced, using journaling to steer my course. Today we talk and journal together about everything. On a practical level, I use an app on my iPad called Penzu for my journaling, but pencil and paper work just as well.

Whatever way you choose to work your walk, don't settle for less than God's best. A dry, spiritless prayer life is so far removed from God's ideal for you that you should literally rebuke even the thought that it would be that way for you.

One more thing with regard to listening. Stop trying so hard! A sure fire intimacy killer in spiritual things is the fire and fury of our own fleshly efforts to produce spiritual results.

Rest is the atmosphere and environment in which His voice is most clearly heard. Not necessarily natural rest, but a serenity of spirit that has ceased striving to please God or *make* things happen, and instead by faith has accepted His abundant provision.

Hebrews 4 is by far one of my favorite chapters in all of Scripture.

"There remaineth therefore a rest to the people of God. For he that is entered into his rest, he also hath ceased from his own works, as God did from his.
Let us labor therefore to enter into that rest, lest any man fall after the same example of unbelief."
Hebrews 4:9–11 KJV

The context of this is found in verse 4, *"Today, if you will hear his voice…"*

Papa wants to speak to you today!

Are you listening?

Have you closed the door on other things to give Him opportunity?

From 'Discovering and Developing a Secret Life of Prayer' by David Lee Martin, available on Amazon

DATE:

THANKYOU, LORD...

THE WORD

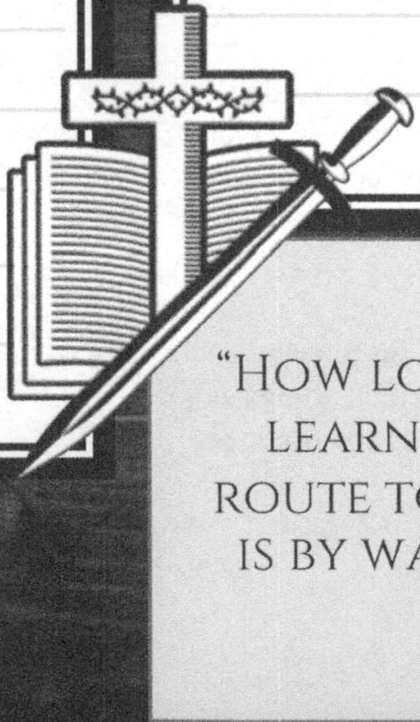

"HOW LONG WILL IT TAKE US TO
LEARN THAT OUR SHORTEST
ROUTE TO THE MAN NEXT DOOR
IS BY WAY OF GOD'S THRONE?"
-A. T. PIERSON

BUT THOU, WHEN THOU PRAYEST, ENTER INTO THY CLOSET,
AND WHEN THOU HAST SHUT THY DOOR, PRAY TO THY
FATHER WHICH IS IN SECRET; AND THY FATHER WHICH
SEETH IN SECRET SHALL REWARD THEE OPENLY.

– Matthew 6:6

DATE:

THANKYOU, LORD...

THE WORD

"MIGHTY MOVES OF GOD BEGIN WITH MIGHTY MOVEMENTS OF THE HEART."
-DAVID LEE MARTIN

YOUR FATHER KNOWETH WHAT THINGS
YE HAVE NEED OF, BEFORE YE ASK HIM.

— Matthew 6:8

DATE:

THANKYOU, LORD...

THE WORD

"IF ADDED POWER ATTENDS THE UNITED PRAYER OF TWO OR THREE, WHAT MIGHTY TRIUMPHS THERE WILL BE WHEN HUNDREDS OF THOUSANDS OF CONSISTENT MEMBERS OF THE CHURCH ARE WITH ONE ACCORD DAY BY DAY MAKING INTERCESSION FOR THE EXTENSION OF CHRIST'S KINGDOM."
-JOHN R. MOTT

BUT THE END OF ALL THINGS IS AT HAND:
BE YE THEREFORE SOBER, AND WATCH UNTO PRAYER

— 1 Peter 4:7

DATE:

THANKYOU, LORD...

THE WORD

"GOD HAS A GOOD DEAL MORE TO GIVE THAN MOST OF US ARE GETTING. "KNEE-OLOGY" IS A MUCH-NEGLECTED BRANCH OF CHRISTIAN ETHICS. THE CHURCH LOSES IMMEASURABLY IN STRENGTH AND ACCELERATED POWER BY FAILING TO TEST THE WONDERFUL PROMISES OF GOD IN PRAYER. OH, FOR SOMEBODY WHO CAN REALLY PRAY."
- C. E. CORNELL

THE EYES OF THE LORD ARE UPON THE RIGHTEOUS,
AND HIS EARS ARE OPEN UNTO THEIR CRY.

— Psalms 34:15

DATE:

THANKYOU, LORD...

THE WORD

"PRAYER ALONE WILL
OVERCOME THE GIGANTIC
DIFFICULTIES WHICH
CONFRONT THE WORKERS IN
EVERY FIELD."
-JOHN R. MOTT

THE LORD IS NIGH UNTO THEM THAT ARE OF A BROKEN
HEART; AND SAVETH SUCH AS BE OF A CONTRITE SPIRIT.

- Psalms 34:18

DATE:

THANKYOU, LORD...

THE WORD

IT MUST BE REMEMBERED THAT
THERE IS SPIRITUAL WICKEDNESS
AT THE BACK OF ALL CONFUSION
AND DISCORD IN THE WORK OF
GOD. THE SERVANT OF CHRIST
MUST, THEREFORE, PRACTICALLY
RECOGNIZE THAT HIS WARFARE IS
WITH THESE SATANIC BEINGS
AND MUST BE WAGED
ON HIS KNEES.."
-D. E. HOSTE

CONTINUE IN PRAYER, AND WATCH IN
THE SAME WITH THANKSGIVING.

– Colossians 4:2

DATE:

THANKYOU, LORD...

THE WORD

"OH CHRISTIANS, GO MORE TO
THE PRAYER-MEETINGS."
-BROWNLOW NORTH

MY HELP COMETH FROM THE LORD,
WHICH MADE HEAVEN AND EARTH.

- Psalms 121:2

DATE:

THANKYOU, LORD...

THE WORD

"THE NEGLECTED HEART WILL SOON BE A HEART OVERRUN WITH WORLDLY THOUGHTS; THE NEGLECTED LIFE WILL SOON BECOME A MORAL CHAOS; THE CHURCH THAT IS NOT JEALOUSLY PROTECTED BY MIGHTY INTERCESSION AND SACRIFICIAL LABORS WILL BEFORE LONG BECOME THE ABODE OF EVERY EVIL BIRD AND THE HIDING PLACE FOR UNSUSPECTED CORRUPTION. THE CREEPING WILDERNESS WILL SOON TAKE OVER THAT CHURCH THAT TRUSTS IN ITS OWN STRENGTH AND FORGETS TO WATCH AND PRAY.." -A. W. TOZER

I HAVE CALLED UPON THEE, FOR THOU WILT HEAR ME, O
GOD: INCLINE THINE EAR UNTO ME, AND HEAR MY SPEECH

— Psalms 17:6

HE *restores* MY *soul*

PSALM 23:3

"LORD, TEACH US TO PRAY"

Jesus' answer to His disciples' question about how to pray is very interesting. Fellowship with the Father was Jesus' major preoccupation so we might expect several chapters of principles concerning this vital subject.

Instead, a simple few lines of instruction are given.
"So He said to them, "When you pray, say:
Our Father in heaven,
Hallowed be Your name.
Your kingdom come. Your will be done on earth as it is in heaven.
Give us day by day our daily bread.
And forgive us our sins, as we also forgive everyone who is indebted to us.
And do not lead us into temptation, but deliver us from the evil one."" *Luke 11:2-4*

The same prayer format is duplicated in *Matt 6:9-13*:
"In this manner, therefore, pray:
Our Father in heaven,
Hallowed be Your name.
Your kingdom come.
Your will be done
On earth as it is in heaven.
Give us this day our daily bread.
And forgive us our trespasses,
As we forgive those who trespass against us.
And do not lead us into temptation,
But deliver us from the evil one.
For Yours is the kingdom and the power and the glory forever. Amen."

So simple.

Eleven lines from the mouth of God that open all of Heaven to His lovers.

I believe that the reason Jesus did not give a detailed outline is because Papa wants each of His children to know the thrill of discovery for themselves.

Religions, including much of what parades itself as Christianity, are crammed with empty repetitions and endless rituals. Jesus left no room for such rubbish!

He gave us a skeleton prayer here, knowing that *the flesh of relationship must be put on the bones of method* for it to become life-giving. Simply put, Jesus did not want to dictate a mechanical methodology that human flesh alone could robotically rehearse. Prayer is after all more about relationship with a Person than it is to do with exercise of a principle. The muscle and sinews of spiritual strength are won in the closet, behind closed doors. The prayer gym is not one full of posers, it's a private and very personal coaching by the King Himself, hidden from the world.

Really the prayer that was given to the followers of Jesus, could better be described as the disciple's prayer. For simplicity, let's just call it *the Prayer*. [*in Acts 1:14 where the scripture records that the disciples gathered in the upper room and continued in one accord in prayer, the actual Greek reads, "they joined together constantly in "the Prayer" and supplication". Other ancient Jewish literature also often refers to the Lord's Prayer as 'the Prayer'*]

In my years studying the subject of prayer, questioning countless other believers and leaders about how and what they pray, and most importantly praying myself, I know for certain that Jesus was not suggesting that we parrot the words of this written prayer and walk away thinking we have prayed.

The Prayer is so much more than this!

I have heard the Prayer described in many ways; hooks on which hang our petitions; a track around which we run.

For me, the picture I see when I consider the Lord's Prayer is a corridor with several doors on each side. One door has the words, 'Our Father' written on it, another 'Hallowed be thy name" and so on.

Each door can be opened and we, as believers in Jesus' name (the key that opens all realms to God's lovers), can freely step through to enjoy encounters with our Savior, our Father and His glorious Holy Spirit. Hours of engaging fellowship, Holy Spirit inspired revelation, and close communion await. Jesus stands at the threshold of each door, warmly ushering us through to these heavenly realities.

Each line of the Prayer is a doorway to a vast and satisfying realm of relationship, each with its own store of promises to bestow…

From 'Discovering and Developing the Secret Depths of the Lord's Prayer' by David Lee Martin, available on Amazon

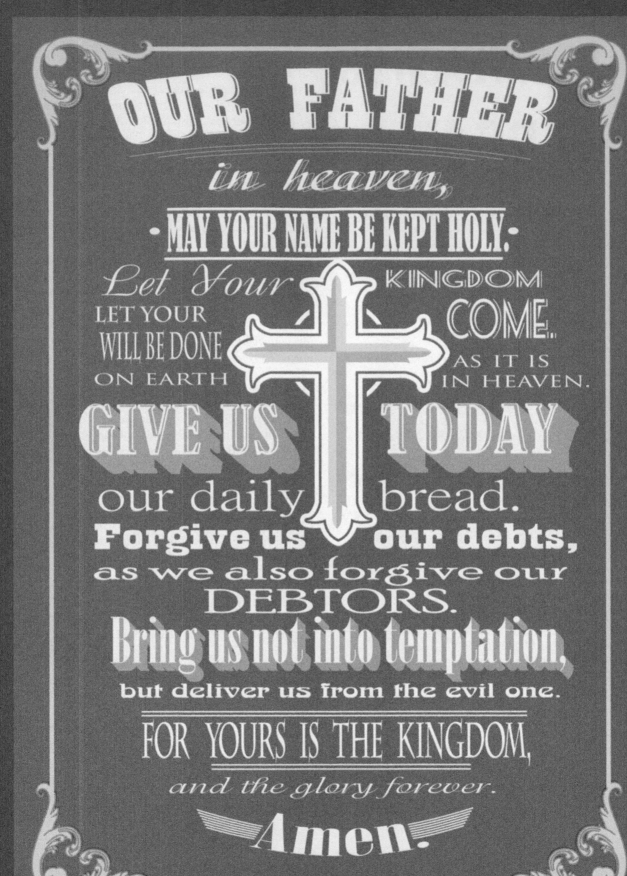

THE LORD'S PRAYER PATHWAY

OUR FATHER IN HEAVEN

This is where we simply acknowledge God as our Father. Through the blood of Jesus we have been brought into right relationship with God and have absolute liberty to approach Him without fear or condemnation.

Take time to thank God for His Son, and for the Blood of Jesus that has made this relationship possible. This alone is very powerful because as you thank God for the Blood you are essentially declaring into the spiritual realm your Covenant with Him. Through the Covenant you have obtained freedom from the curse.

Take time to thank God for this spiritual and mental freedom that Christ has obtained for you, and for physical healing in your body.

Take opportunity to humble my heart before God. He is indeed in Heaven, high and lifted up. He is the Holy One, on the throne, and without equal.

He is the Potter, and we are the clay. He is the Shepherd and we are the sheep. As we give place to the Father, and recognise our inability and helplessness without Him or His Spirit, the presence of God is drawn to us. Just as Jesus pointed to the sinner not the Pharisee as an example of prayer in Luke 18:9-14, so His heart and presence will be drawn not to a proud heart but to one of humility:

"The LORD is near to those who have a broken heart, And saves such as have a contrite spirit." (Psalms 34:18 NKJV)

HALLOWED BE THY NAME

Hallowing or setting apart as special the Name of God is more than just a pretty praise time, it is a declaration of what He IS and WILL BE to you in your life. As we praise God our righteousness, His righteousness is imparted to us. As we exalt Him as our Victory banner, the overcoming victorious Spirit of God is drawn to us and released within us. Everything in this prayer is alive and active – it is not just a dead framework or form.

THY KINGDOM COME,
THY WILL BE DONE ON EARTH AS IT IS IN HEAVEN

Declare and call for the will of God to be done. At times we will be asking the Father for His hand in the affairs of our life or the lives of others, at other times we will take these words as commands and exercise the authority we have been given in Christ. Just as Christ commanded the storm to "Be Still!" so we can command in certain situation, "Will of God BE DONE!", "Kingdom of God, COME AND BE ESTABLISHED!"

As we pray we conform our own life and thinking to agree with His Word, and partner with the Father to see His will established here on earth. Our words become creative missiles (Proverbs 18:21) and spiritual power is released into the situations we pray for.

GIVE US THIS DAY OUR DAILY BREAD

Philippians 4:6-7 tells us to let all of our requests be made to God. It is here that we are able to bring specific needs to our Father's attention, knowing that as we ask according to His will He will answer and grant the very thing we have asked

"And this is the confidence (the assurance, the privilege of boldness) which we have in Him: [we are sure] that if we ask anything (make any request) according to His will (in agreement with His own plan), He listens to and hears us. And if (since) we [positively] know that He listens to us in whatever we ask, we also know [with settled and absolute knowledge] that we have [granted us as our present possessions] the requests made of Him." (1John 5:14-15 AMP)

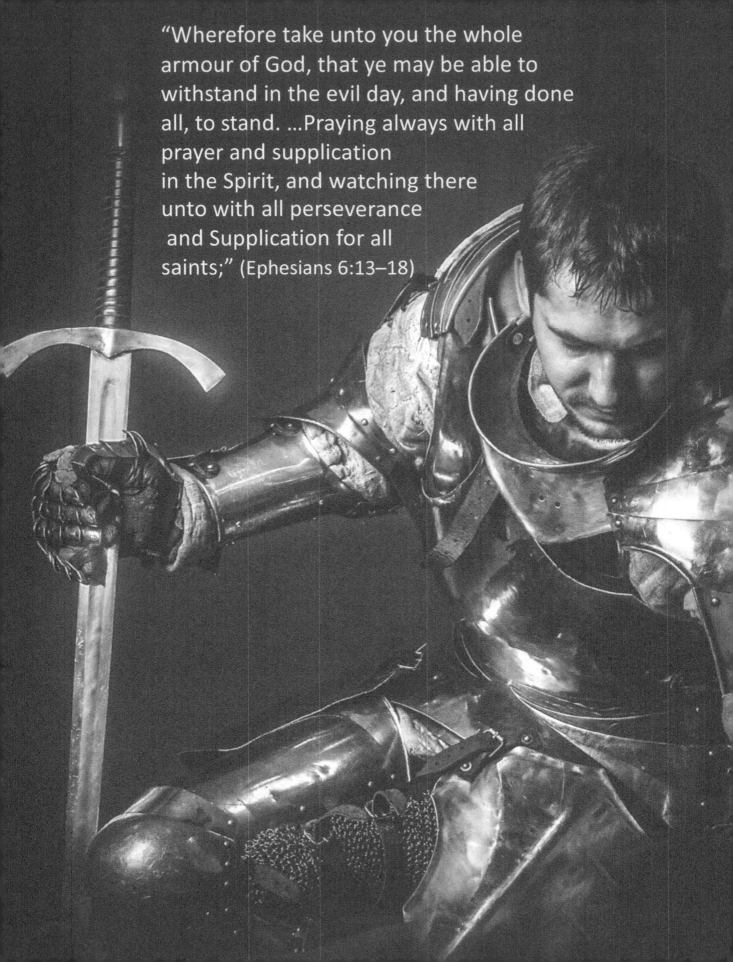

"Wherefore take unto you the whole armour of God, that ye may be able to withstand in the evil day, and having done all, to stand. ...Praying always with all prayer and supplication in the Spirit, and watching there unto with all perseverance and Supplication for all saints;" (Ephesians 6:13–18)

FORGIVE US OUR SINS AS WE FORGIVE THOSE WHO SIN AGAINST US.

Clean hands and a pure heart are essential to confident prayer. John the Apostle speaks of this when he couples the conscience with our ability to confidently receive from Heaven:

"For if our heart condemn us, God is greater than our heart, and knoweth all things. Beloved, if our heart condemn us not, then have we confidence toward God. And whatsoever we ask, we receive of him, because we keep his commandments, and do those things that are pleasing in his sight." *(1John 3:20-22 KJV)*

Jesus also stressed the importance of a heart free of malice or unforgiveness in regard to effective prayer:

"And when ye stand praying, forgive, if ye have ought against any: that your Father also which is in heaven may forgive you your trespasses. But if ye do not forgive, neither will your Father which is in heaven forgive your trespasses." *(Mark 11:25-26 KJV)*

Search and cleanse your heart of any thing that may hinder your answer being granted and your receiving. The price of holding on to bitterness and unforgiveness is just too great, so we intelligently keep short accounts, and continually ensure we are in the love of God and fulfilling God's command to love others (even if at times they are not loving us).

LEAD US NOT INTO TEMPTATION – DELIVER US FROM EVIL

Satan is always prowling around seeking to devour those whom he finds exposed and venerable. We are warned not to think more highly of ourselves than we ought, but to think soberly. We are but flesh and blood, and we too need God's grace to walk uprightly.

Temptation can come in many guises, but if we keep our heart sensitive and vigilant we will be able to overcome any temptation or test that comes our way *(1 Cor 10:13)*. Each day we clothe ourselves with Christ, the armour of light *(Rom 13:12-14; Eph 6:14-17)*, and consciously tuck ourselves under the wing of God.

Position yourself to overcome, and walk in the blessing of the Most High.

FOR THINE IS THE KINGDOM, THE POWER AND THE GLORY, FOREVER AND EVER.

Just as we began by recognising and exalting the Father, so we end our prayers rejoicing in His greatness and victory. We recognise His Kingdom rule in our lives, His power at work in and through us, and His glory above all else.

More than that, it is forever and ever – we now have an eternal perspective on things, having been lifted into His presence, knowing and sensing that we are seated with Christ in heavenly places.

Truly, the Lord's Prayer puts things in their proper place and perspective, positioning us for blessing, and powerfully releasing God's grace into the world around us.

AMEN!

DATE:

THANKYOU, LORD...

THE WORD

"LIVE NEAR TO GOD, AND SO ALL THINGS WILL APPEAR TO YOU LITTLE IN COMPARISON WITH ETERNAL REALITIES."
-ROBERT MURRAY

KEEP ME AS THE APPLE OF THE EYE, HIDE ME
UNDER THE SHADOW OF THY WINGS

– Psalms 17:7-8

DATE:

THANKYOU, LORD...

THE WORD

"THE CHURCH HAS NOT YET TOUCHED THE FRINGE OF THE POSSIBILITIES OF INTERCESSORY PRAYER. HER LARGEST VICTORIES WILL BE WITNESSED WHEN INDIVIDUAL CHRISTIANS EVERYWHERE COME TO RECOGNIZE THEIR PRIESTHOOD UNTO GOD AND DAY BY DAY GIVE THEMSELVES UNTO PRAYER."
-JOHN R. MOTT

IF YE THEN, BEING EVIL, KNOW HOW TO GIVE GOOD GIFTS UNTO
YOUR CHILDREN, HOW MUCH MORE SHALL YOUR FATHER WHICH
IS IN HEAVEN GIVE GOOD THINGS TO THEM THAT ASK HIM?

– Matthew 7:11

DATE:

THANKYOU, LORD...

THE WORD

THE EVANGELIZATION OF THE
WORLD IN THIS GENERATION
DEPENDS FIRST OF ALL UPON A
REVIVAL OF PRAYER. DEEPER
THAN THE NEED FOR MEN;
DEEPER, FAR, THAN THE NEED
FOR MONEY; AYE, DEEP DOWN
AT THE BOTTOM OF OUR
SPIRITLESS LIFE IS THE NEED FOR
THE FORGOTTEN SECRET OF
PREVAILING, WORLD-WIDE
PRAYER.."
-ROBERT E. SPEER

TAKE YE HEED, WATCH AND PRAY: FOR
YE KNOW NOT WHEN THE TIME IS.

— Mark 13:33

DATE:

THANKYOU, LORD...

THE WORD

> "FAITH AND PRAYER ARE SO
> INTER-LINKED THAT FAITH IS
> PRAYER AND PRAYER IS FAITH.
> YOU CANNOT SEPARATE THEM.
> YOU COULD NOT HAVE THE ONE
> WITHOUT THE OTHER."
> -A. LINDSAY GLEGG

WHO IN THE DAYS OF HIS FLESH, WHEN HE HAD OFFERED UP
PRAYERS AND SUPPLICATIONS WITH STRONG CRYING AND
TEARS UNTO HIM THAT WAS ABLE TO SAVE HIM FROM
DEATH, AND WAS HEARD IN THAT HE FEARED.

—Hebrews 5:7

DATE:

THANKYOU, LORD...

"I BELIEVE THERE IS ONE THING FOR WHICH GOD IS VERY ANGRY WITH OUR LAND, AND FOR WHICH HIS HOLY SPIRIT IS SO LITTLE AMONG US, AND THAT IS THE NEGLECT OF UNITED PRAYER; THE APPOINTED MEANS OF BRINGING DOWN THE HOLY SPIRIT."
-BROWNLOW NORTH

IS ANY AMONG YOU AFFLICTED? LET HIM PRAY.
IS ANY MERRY? LET HIM SING PSALMS.

– *James 5:13*

JESUS SAID
come
UNTO ME
I WILL GIVE YOU
rest

Matthew 11.28

DATE:

THANKYOU, LORD...

THE WORD

"THE NEGLECT OF PRAYER PROVES TO MY MIND, THAT THERE IS A LARGE AMOUNT OF PRACTICAL INFIDELITY. IF THE PEOPLE BELIEVED THAT THERE WAS A REAL, EXISTING, PERSONAL GOD, THEY WOULD ASK HIM FOR WHAT THEY WANTED, AND THEY WOULD GET WHAT THEY ASKED. BUT THEY DO NOT ASK, BECAUSE THEY DO NOT BELIEVE OR EXPECT TO RECEIVE." - BROWNLOW NORTH

AND SHE WAS A WIDOW OF ABOUT FOURSCORE AND FOUR
YEARS, WHICH DEPARTED NOT FROM THE TEMPLE, BUT SERVED
GOD WITH FASTINGS AND PRAYERS NIGHT AND DAY..
~ Luke 2:37

DATE:

THANKYOU, LORD...

THE WORD

"PRAYER IS SELF-DISCIPLINE. THE EFFORT TO REALIZE THE PRESENCE AND POWER OF GOD STRETCHES THE SINEWS OF THE SOUL AND HARDENS ITS MUSCLES. TO PRAY IS TO GROW IN GRACE. TO TARRY IN THE PRESENCE OF THE KING LEADS TO NEW LOYALTY AND DEVOTION ON THE PART OF THE FAITHFUL SUBJECTS. CHRISTIAN CHARACTER GROWS IN THE SECRET-PLACE OF PRAYER."
-SAMUEL M. ZWEMER

IF YE ABIDE IN ME, AND MY WORDS ABIDE IN YOU, YE SHALL ASK WHAT YE WILL, AND IT SHALL BE DONE UNTO YOU.

– John 15:7

DATE:

THANKYOU, LORD...

THE WORD

"WE HAVE NOT BEEN MEN OF PRAYER. THE SPIRIT OF PRAYER HAS SLUMBERED AMONG US. THE CLOSET HAS BEEN TOO LITTLE FREQUENTED AND DELIGHTED IN. WE HAVE ALLOWED BUSINESS, STUDY OR ACTIVE LABOR TO INTERFERE WITH OUR CLOSET-HOURS. AND THE FEVERISH ATMOSPHERE IN WHICH BOTH THE CHURCH AND THE NATION ARE ENVELOPED HAS FOUND ITS WAY INTO OUR PRAYER CLOSETS."
-ANDREW BONAR

LET US THEREFORE COME BOLDLY UNTO THE THRONE OF
GRACE, THAT WE MAY OBTAIN MERCY, AND FIND GRACE TO
HELP IN TIME OF NEED.

- Hebrews 4:16

DATE:

THANKYOU, LORD...

THE WORD

"WHY IS THERE SO LITTLE FORETHOUGHT IN THE LAYING OUT OF TIME AND EMPLOYMENT, SO AS SECURE A LARGE PORTION OF EACH DAY FOR PRAYER? WHY IS THERE SO MUCH SPEAKING, YET SO LITTLE PRAYER? WHY IS THERE SO MUCH RUNNING TO AND FRO TO MEETINGS, CONVENTIONS, FELLOWSHIP GATHERINGS AND YET SO LITTLE TIME FOR PRAYER'? BRETHREN, WHY SO MANY MEETINGS WITH OUR FELLOW MEN AND SO FEW MEETINGS WITH GOD?
-ANDREW BONAR

LET MY PRAYER BE SET FORTH BEFORE THEE AS INCENSE; AND
THE LIFTING UP OF MY HANDS AS THE EVENING SACRIFICE.

— Psalms 141:2

DATE:

THANKYOU, LORD...

THE WORD

"TRUE PRAYER WILL ACHIEVE JUST AS MUCH AS IT COSTS US."
-SAMUEL M. ZWEMER

O SATISFY US EARLY WITH THY MERCY; THAT WE MAY
REJOICE AND BE GLAD ALL OUR DAYS.
— *Psalms 90:14*

DATE:

THANKYOU, LORD...

THE WORD

"GOD HAS NO GREATER
CONTROVERSY WITH HIS
PEOPLE TODAY THAN THIS,
THAT WITH BOUNDLESS
PROMISES TO BELIEVING
PRAYER, THERE ARE SO FEW
WHO ACTUALLY GIVE
THEMSELVES UNTO
INTERCESSION."
-A. T. PIERSON

O GOD, THOU ART MY GOD;   EARLY WILL I SEEK THEE: MY
SOUL THIRSTETH FOR THEE, MY FLESH LONGETH FOR THEE
IN A DRY AND THIRSTY LAND, WHERE NO WATER IS.

— *Psalms 63:1*

DATE:

THANKYOU, LORD...

THE WORD

"YOU MUST PRAY WITH ALL YOUR MIGHT. THAT DOES NOT MEAN SAYING YOUR PRAYERS, OR SITTING GAZING ABOUT IN CHURCH OR CHAPEL WITH EYES WIDE OPEN WHILE SOMEONE ELSE SAYS THEM FOR YOU. IT MEANS FERVENT, EFFECTUAL, UNTIRING WRESTLING WITH GOD...THIS KIND OF PRAYER BE SURE THE DEVIL AND THE WORLD AND YOUR OWN INDOLENT, UNBELIEVING NATURE WILL OPPOSE. THEY WILL POUR WATER ON THIS FLAME."
-WILLIAM BOOTH

AND ALL THINGS, WHATSOEVER YE SHALL ASK IN PRAYER,
BELIEVING, YE SHALL RECEIVE.
– Matthew 21:22

DATE:

THANKYOU, LORD...

THE WORD

"WHAT A MAN IS ON HIS KNEES
BEFORE GOD IN SECRET, THAT
WILL HE BE BEFORE MEN: THAT
MUCH AND NO MORE."
- FRED MITCHELL

AND IN THE MORNING, RISING UP A GREAT WHILE BEFORE
DAY, HE WENT OUT, AND DEPARTED INTO A SOLITARY
PLACE, AND THERE PRAYED.
– Mark 1:35

DATE:

THANKYOU, LORD...

THE WORD

"AT WATERLOO, THE ENGLISH
TROOPS OBEYING ORDERS FELL
ON THEIR FACES FOR A TIME
AND LET THE HOT FIRE OF THE
FRENCH ARTILLERY PASS OVER
THEM. THEN THEY SPRANG TO
THEIR FEET AND RUSHED TO
THE THICKEST OF THE FIGHT
AND BEAT BACK THEIR FOES.
THE LORD WANTS HIS PEOPLE
FLAT ON THEIR FACES, BEFORE
THEY ATTEMPT TO MEET THE
GREAT CRISES OF LIFE."
-A. T. PIERSON

WHEREFORE ALSO WE PRAY ALWAYS FOR YOU, THAT OUR
GOD WOULD COUNT YOU WORTHY OF THIS CALLING, AND
FULFIL ALL THE GOOD PLEASURE OF HIS GOODNESS, AND
THE WORK OF FAITH WITH POWER.

– 2 Thessalonians 1:11

LOVE YOURSELF LIKE JESUS LOVES YOU
- RADICALLY & WITH ALL YOUR HEART -

"Master, which is the great commandment in the law? Jesus said unto him, Thou shalt love the Lord thy God with all thy heart, and with all thy soul, and with all thy mind. This is the first and great commandment. And the second is like unto it, Thou shalt love thy neighbor as thyself. On these two commandments hang all the law and the prophets." *(Matthew 22:36–40 KJV)*

Here we have Jesus' own statement revealing the heart of God's commandments.

It is a three-legged stool. If you lose one of the legs you will topple over. It is very difficult to truly love, accept, celebrate and champion the good in others when you see no good in yourself.

The three legs of the stool all bear weight and make for a stable and balanced life that is lived fully and without a lopsided slant that skews perception and perspective. With three legs intact, our thoughts, words and actions flow from wholeness rather than a hole!

Throughout my years of pastoring I have seen this phenomenon again and again. But I'm not going to hide behind the pastor's hat and make out that my perceptions were honed by the issues of other people. The closest and most poignant example of someone living from their inner woundedness is the handsome man who looks back at me from the mirror each morning.

What you are deeply seeking from others, be it affirmation, affection, acceptance - are you giving these things to yourself? Actively, intentionally and with absolute conviction and passionate agreement with Papa's Words over you?

Jesus' commandment has three important legs that everything else is held up by.

Love God!

Yep, we get that one. Super important! Most believers agree wholeheartedly that our zeal and love for God should characterize our lives.

Love your neighbor.

A bit more challenging, but most agree that this is essential too. Many times we feel guilty for not really fulfilling this commandment as well as we would like to. We try hard and so often fail. But the problem may not be rooted in our inability to love other people so much as in what precedes actively and honestly loving the people around us.

It is a tiny (but massive) detail that can easily be overlooked or conveniently ignored.

You are called to love others "…as thyself."

Love Thyself!

Our drive to survive certainly reveals a level of self-love (or at the very least self-preservation), but, beyond that, deep down, many people struggle with even the idea of genuinely loving themselves because they feel so unlovable. The messages they have received throughout their lives have compounded the belief that they don't quite measure up.

But our Papa says:

Love yourself.
Accept yourself.
Support yourself.
Encourage yourself.
Delight in yourself.
Celebrate yourself.
Recognize and affirm the good in yourself.
Enjoy yourself.
Defend and protect yourself from the devil's lies.

One of the simplest but most profoundly life-changing truths is found in John chapter 16:

"For the Father himself loveth you…"
John 16:27 KJV

129

He is a good Father, and one who gives good gifts. Do you honestly think that Papa is whipping you everyday with those accusing thoughts? Of course He's not!

Instead of agreeing with the devil's whispers that you are a loser, chase that scoundrel from your sphere like you would chase an angry hornet. Be the angry hornet times 10 and scare the stinger out of him! All of those fork-tongued barbs he wants to throw at you? Throw them back, returned to sender! Instead of bowing your head in shame when he suggests that you are unloved and unlovable, unwanted and underwhelming, kick his rear-end with the Word of God and your agreement with God's blood-bought declaration over you, "I am loved!"

"I love God!"
"I love myself!"
"I love others!"

Your point of agreement should no longer be with your failings but with His victory. You were bought with a price.

The value of something is measured by the price someone is willing to pay to acquire it. What price was Papa happy to pay for you?

Excerpt from *Love Yourself Like Jesus Loves You – Radically & With All Your Heart* by David Lee Martin

CONSIDER AND SPEAK OUT WHAT THE LORD SAYS IN HIS WORD ABOUT YOUR NEW IDENTITY IN CHRIST JESUS...

IN CHRIST SCRIPTURES

God tells me in His word that...

I AM God's child for I am born again of the incorruptible seed of the Word of God which lives and abides forever. 1Pet 1:23

I AM Forgiven of all my sins. 1Jn2:12 1Jn 1:9

I AM A new creature. 2 Cor 5:17

I AM The temple of the Holy Spirit. 1 Cor6:19

I AM Delivered from the power of darkness and translated into God's Kingdom. Col 1: 13

I AM Redeemed from the curse of the law. 1 Pet 1:18,19; Gal 3:13

I AM Blessed! Deut 28:2; Gal 3:9

I AM the head and not the tail. Above only and not beneath. Deut 28:13

I AM holy and without blame before Him in love. Eph 1:4

I AM Established to the end. 1 Cor 1:8

I AM made near by the blood of Jesus. Eph 2:13

I AM Victorious. 1 Cor 15: 57

I AM set free. Jn 8:36

I AM Strong in the Lord. Eph 6:10

I AM dead to sin and alive to God. Rom 6:11

I AM More than a conqueror. Rom 8:37

I AM joint heir with Christ. Rom 8:17

I AM The light of the world. Mat 5:14

I AM the salt of the earth. Mat5:13

I AM The righteousness of God. 2 Cor 5:21

I AM Called of God. 2 Tim 1:9

I AM Complete in Him. Col 2:10

I AM crucified with Christ. Gal 2:20

I AM Alive with Christ. Eph 2:4,5

I AM Sealed with the Holy Spirit of Promise. Eph 1 :13

I AM a son of God. Gal 4:7

I AM In Christ Jesus, by His doing. 1 Cor 1 :30

I AM accepted in the Beloved. Eph 1:6

I AM a partaker of His divine nature. 2 Pet 1:4

I AM free from condemnation. Rom 8:1

I AM Reconciled to God. 2 Cor 5:18

I AM qualified to share in His inheritance. Col 1 :12

I AM Firmly rooted, built up, established in my faith and over flowing with gratitude. Col 2:7

I AM A fellow citizen with the saints and of the household of God. Eph 2:19

I AM Built upon the foundation of the apostles & prophets, Jesus Christ Himself being the Chief Corner Stone. Eph 2:20

> "God's plan is to make much of the man, far more of him than of anything else. Men are God's method. The Church is looking for better methods; God is looking for better men."
> **E.M. Bounds**
> **Power Through Prayer**

I AM born of God and the evil one does not touch me. 1 Jn5:18

I AM His faithful follower. Eph 5:1

I AM raised up with Christ and seated in heavenly places. Eph 2:6

I AM beloved of God. Col 3:12

I AM One in Christ .Jn 17:21

I AM overtaken with blessings. Eph 1:3

I AM His disciple because I have love for others. Jn 13:34,35

I AM the firstfruits among His creation. James 1 :18

I AM Chosen. Eph1:4

I AM an ambassador for Christ. 2 Cor 5:20

I AM God's workmanship created in Christ Jesus for good works. Eph 2:10

I AM the apple of my Father's eye. Ps 17:8

I AM Healed by the stripes of Jesus. 1 Pet 2:24

I AM being changed into His image. 2 Cor 3:18

I AM a true worshiper who worships the Father in Spirit and in Truth. John 4:24

I AM free from fear because the perfect love of God within me casts out all fear! 1 John 4:18

I AM without sin. 1John 3:9

I AM changed into the exact image of Jesus. 2Cor 3:18

I AM as Jesus is right now and forever! 1 John 4:17

I AM the redeemed of the Lord, redeemed from the hand of the enemy. Psalm 107:2

I HAVE The mind of Christ. 1 Cor 2:16

I HAVE obtained an inheritance. Eph 1 :11

I HAVE Access by one Spirit to the Father. Eph 2:18

I HAVE overcome the world. 1 Jn 5:4

I HAVE Everlasting life and will not be condemned. Jn 5:24

I HAVE God as my heavenly Father. 2 Cor 6:18

I HAVE the Spirit of wisdom and revelation in the knowledge of Him. Eph 1:17

I HAVE The peace of God which passes understanding. Phil 4:7

I HAVE Received power, the power of the Holy Spirit; power to lay hands on
the sick and see them recover; power to cast out demons. Mk 16:17,18

I HAVE Authority over all the power of the enemy, and nothing shall by any means hurt me.
Luke 10:19

I LIVE by and in the law of the Spirit of life in Christ Jesus. Rom 8:2

I WALK In Christ Jesus. Col 2:6

I CAN do all things in Christ Jesus. Phil 4:13

I CAN come boldly to the throne of grace. Hebrews 4:16

MY LIFE Is hidden with Christ in God. Col 3:3

I SHALL do even greater works than Christ Jesus. Jn 14:12

The Greater One in me is greater than he who is in the world. 1 Jn 4:4

I Always triumph in Christ. 2 Cor 2:14

I proclaim and show forth His praise. 1 Pet 2:9

I Overcome evil with good. Rom 12:21

I put my faith in the power of God. 1 Cor 2:5

I PRESS toward the mark for the prize of the high calling of God. Phil 3: 14

GOD is directing my paths. Prov 3:5,6

DATE:

THANKYOU, LORD...

THE WORD

"A MARBLE CUTTER, WITH CHISEL AND HAMMER, WAS CHANGING A STONE INTO A STATUE. A PREACHER LOOKING ON SAID: 'I WISH I COULD DEAL SUCH CHANGING BLOWS ON STONY HEARTS. THE WORKMAN ANSWERED: 'MAYBE YOU COULD, IF YOU WORKED LIKE ME, UPON YOUR KNEE."
-A. T. PIERSON

CALL UNTO ME, AND I WILL ANSWER THEE, AND SHEW THEE
GREAT AND MIGHTY THINGS, WHICH THOU KNOWEST NOT.

- *Jeremiah 33:3*

DATE:

THANKYOU, LORD...

THE WORD

> "IT IS MORALLY IMPOSSIBLE TO EXERCISE TRUST IN GOD WHILE THERE IS FAILURE TO WAIT UPON HIM FOR GUIDANCE AND DIRECTION. THE MAN WHO DOES NOT LEARN TO WAIT UPON THE LORD AND HAVE HIS THOUGHTS MOLDED BY HIM WILL NEVER POSSESS THAT STEADY PURPOSE AND CALM TRUST, WHICH IS ESSENTIAL TO THE EXERCISE OF WISE INFLUENCE UPON OTHERS, IN TIMES OF CRISIS AND DIFFICULTY."
> - D. E. HOSTE

PRAYING ALWAYS WITH ALL PRAYER AND SUPPLICATION IN
THE SPIRIT, AND WATCHING THEREUNTO WITH ALL
PERSEVERANCE AND SUPPLICATION FOR ALL SAINTS
- *Ephesians 6:18*

WE WALK by Faith NOT BY SIGHT

2 Corinthians 5:7

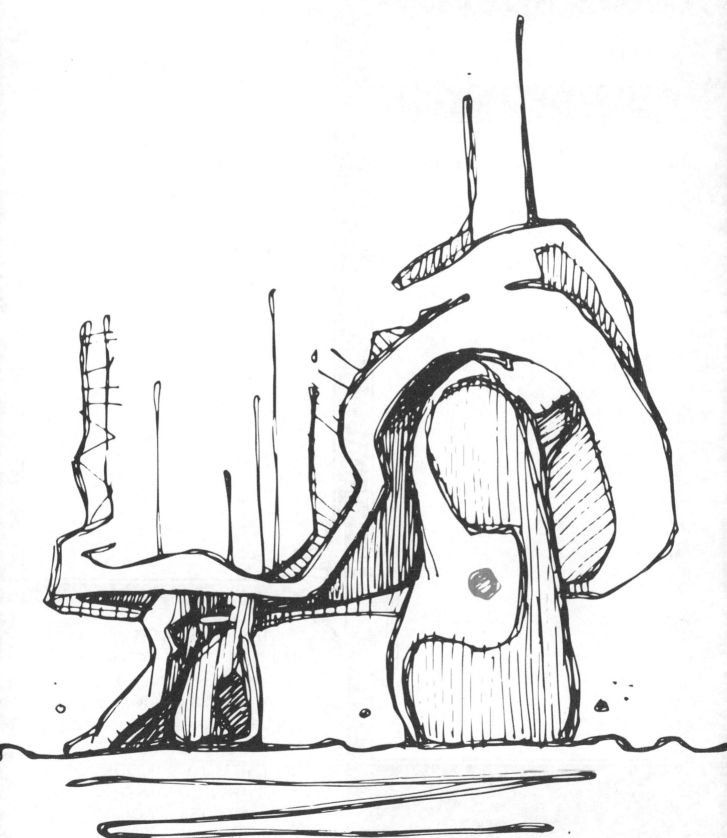

DATE:

THANKYOU, LORD...

THE WORD

"THE GREAT BATTLES, THE
BATTLES THAT DECIDE OUR
DESTINY AND THE DESTINY
OF GENERATIONS YET
UNBORN, ARE NOT FOUGHT
ON PUBLIC PLATFORMS, BUT
IN THE LONELY HOURS OF
THE NIGHT AND IN
MOMENTS OF AGONY."
-SAMUEL LOGAN BRENGLE

FOR WHERE TWO OR THREE ARE GATHERED TOGETHER IN MY
NAME, THERE AM I IN THE MIDST OF THEM.
− Matthew 18:20

DATE:

THANKYOU, LORD...

THE WORD

"A GODLY MAN IS A PRAYING MAN. AS SOON AS GRACE IS POURED IN, PRAYER IS POURED OUT. PRAYER IS THE SOUL'S TRAFFIC WITH HEAVEN; GOD COMES DOWN TO US BY HIS SPIRIT, AND WE GO UP TO HIM BY PRAYER."
-THOMAS WATSON

FINALLY, BRETHREN, PRAY FOR US, THAT THE WORD
OF THE LORD MAY HAVE FREE COURSE, AND BE
GLORIFIED, EVEN AS IT IS WITH YOU.

- 2 Thessalonians 1:11

DATE:

THANKYOU, LORD...

THE WORD

"THE WORD OF GOD REPRESENTS ALL THE POSSIBILITIES OF GOD AS AT THE DISPOSAL OF TRUE PRAYER."
- A. T. PIERSON

143

I WILL THEREFORE THAT MEN PRAY EVERY WHERE, LIFTING
UP HOLY HANDS, WITHOUT WRATH AND DOUBTING.
— 1 Timothy 2:8

DATE:

THANKYOU, LORD...

THE WORD

"WHETHER WE LIKE IT OR
NOT, ASKING IS THE RULE OF
THE KINGDOM. IF YOU MAY
HAVE EVERYTHING BY ASKING
IN HIS NAME, AND NOTHING
WITHOUT ASKING, I BEG YOU
TO SEE HOW ABSOLUTELY
VITAL PRAYER IS."
- C. H. SPURGEON

HENCEFORTH I CALL YOU NOT SERVANTS; FOR THE
SERVANT KNOWETH NOT WHAT HIS LORD DOETH: BUT I
HAVE CALLED YOU FRIENDS; FOR ALL THINGS THAT I HAVE
HEARD OF MY FATHER I HAVE MADE KNOWN UNTO YOU.
- John 15:15

Christ died for our sins

1 Corinthians 15:3

AND BY HIS *wounds* WE ARE *healed*

ISAIAH 53:5

DATE:

THANKYOU, LORD...

THE WORD

"PRAYER – SECRET, FERVENT,
BELIEVING PRAYER – LIES AT
THE ROOT OF ALL
PERSONAL GODLINESS."
- WILLIAM CAREY

THE YOUNG LIONS DO LACK, AND SUFFER HUNGER: BUT THEY
THAT SEEK THE LORD SHALL NOT WANT ANY GOOD THING.

– Psalms 34:10

DATE:

THANKYOU, LORD...

THE WORD

"ALL GREAT SOUL-WINNERS
HAVE BEEN MEN OF MUCH AND
MIGHTY PRAYER, AND ALL
GREAT REVIVALS HAVE BEEN
PRECEDED AND CARRIED OUT
BY PERSEVERING, PREVAILING
KNEE-WORK IN THE CLOSET."
- GORDON COVE

WATCH YE AND PRAY, LEST YE ENTER INTO TEMPTATION.
THE SPIRIT TRULY IS READY, BUT THE FLESH IS WEAK..

— *Mark 14:38*

DATE:

THE WORD

THANKYOU, LORD...

"THE NEGLECT OF PRAYER IS
A GRAND HINDRANCE
TO HOLINESS."
- JOHN WESLEY

NOW WHEN ALL THE PEOPLE WERE BAPTIZED, IT CAME TO
PASS, THAT JESUS ALSO BEING BAPTIZED, AND PRAYING, THE
HEAVEN WAS OPENED..
- *Luke 3:21*

DATE:

THANKYOU, LORD...

THE WORD

"GOD WILL NOT LET ME GET THE BLESSING WITHOUT ASKING. TODAY I AM SETTING MY FACE TO FAST AND PRAY FOR ENLIGHTENMENT AND REFRESHING. UNTIL I CAN GET UP TO THE MEASURE OF AT LEAST TWO HOURS IN PURE PRAYER EVERY DAY, I SHALL NOT BE CONTENTED. MEDITATION AND READING BESIDES."
- ANDREW BONAR

AND HE WITHDREW HIMSELF INTO
THE WILDERNESS, AND PRAYED.
— *Luke 5:16*

DATE:

THANKYOU, LORD...

THE WORD

"BEWARE IN YOUR PRAYERS,
ABOVE EVERYTHING ELSE, OF
LIMITING GOD, NOT ONLY
BY UNBELIEF, BUT BY FANCYING
THAT YOU KNOW WHAT HE
CAN DO. EXPECT UNEXPECTED
THINGS, ABOVE ALL THAT WE
ASK OR THINK. EACH TIME,
BEFORE YOU INTERCEDE, BE
QUIET FIRST, AND WORSHIP
GOD IN HIS GLORY. THINK OF
WHAT HE CAN DO, AND HOW
HE DELIGHTS TO HEAR THE
PRAYERS OF HIS REDEEMED
PEOPLE. THINK OF YOUR PLACE
AND PRIVILEGE IN CHRIST, AND
EXPECT GREAT THINGS!"
- ANDREW MURRAY

AND IT CAME TO PASS IN THOSE DAYS, THAT HE WENT OUT
INTO A MOUNTAIN TO PRAY, AND CONTINUED ALL NIGHT IN
PRAYER TO GOD.
— Luke 6:12

DATE:

THANKYOU, LORD...

THE WORD

"WHEN WE FIND ANYTHING PROMISED IN THE WORD OF GOD, WE ARE NOT TO NEGLECT TO SEEK IT BECAUSE IT IS PROMISED: BUT WE ARE TO PRAY FOR IT ON THAT VERY ACCOUNT. THUS SAITH THE LORD GOD; I WILL YET FOR THIS BE INQUIRED OF BY THE HOUSE OF ISRAEL, TO DO IT FOR THEM; I WILL INCREASE THEM WITH MEN LIKE A FLOCK" (EZEK. 36:37). THE PROMISE IS ABSOLUTE; BUT THE TIME OF ITS FULFILLMENT DEPENDS UPON THE PRAYERS OF HIS PEOPLE."
- ANDREW MURRAY

FOR IT IS SANCTIFIED BY THE WORD OF GOD AND PRAYER.
— 1 Timothy 4:5

For everyone who *asks*

RECEIVES

the one who *seeks*

FINDS

and to the one who

knocks

the door will be

OPENED

Matthew 7:8

RIPPLE PRAYER

Ripple Prayer is when we drop our requests in the pool of God's willingness to answer and act on our behalf. In ever expanding circles, one request leads to another, leading us to bring many areas to the throne of God's grace.

Usually we would start with ourselves, presenting our personal needs and requests before God, then we might pray for our family, close neighbors and friends. This naturally leads us to prayer for families in our area or church, colleagues at work or others in our sphere of influence. We might then pray for other churches in our area, evangelism through the Body of believers in our town, our county or nation, missions work at home and abroad. Maybe then we would pray personally for each individual in our home groups, that they would be effective witnesses in their respective mission fields... And so on as the Spirit leads.

Taking the ripple idea presented in Acts 1:8 you can expand it this way...

Jerusalem

you and your family
church - evangelism

Judea (involvement situation)

school, workplace, neighborhood, town etc

Samaria (known situation)

friends needs, other situations needing God's power

The ends of the earth

World situation - nations, catastrophes, revival, missions

Simply allow God's Holy Spirit to lead you from one area to another. In this way one hour can be filled with ease.

DATE:

THANKYOU, LORD...

THE WORD

> "IF I COULD HEAR CHRIST PRAYING FOR ME IN THE NEXT ROOM, I WOULD NOT FEAR A MILLION ENEMIES. YET DISTANCE MAKES NO DIFFERENCE.
> HE IS PRAYING FOR ME."
> - ANDREW MURRAY

I THANK MY GOD, MAKING MENTION OF
THEE ALWAYS IN MY PRAYERS.
– Philemon 1:4

DATE:

THANKYOU, LORD...

THE WORD

"I WOULD RATHER TEACH
ONE MAN TO PRAY THAN
TEN MEN TO PREACH."
-J. H. JOWETT

THEREFORE I SAY UNTO YOU, WHAT THINGS SOEVER YE
DESIRE, WHEN YE PRAY, BELIEVE THAT YE RECEIVE THEM,
AND YE SHALL HAVE THEM.
– Mark 11:24

DATE:

THANKYOU, LORD...

THE WORD

"Oh, how few find time for prayer! There is time for everything else, time to sleep and time to eat, time to read the newspaper and the novel, time to visit friends, time for everything else under the sun, but-no time for prayer, the most important of all things, the one great essential."
-Oswald Smith

BUT THE END OF ALL THINGS IS AT HAND: BE YE THEREFORE
SOBER, AND WATCH UNTO PRAYER.

— *1 Peter 4:7*

THE WORD

THANKYOU, LORD...

"ON THE MOUNTAINS, TORRENTS FLOW RIGHT ALONG, CUTTING THEIR OWN COURSES. BUT ON THE PLAINS CANALS HAVE TO BE DUG OUT PAINFULLY BY MEN SO THAT THE WATER MIGHT FLOW. SO AMONG THOSE WHO LIVE ON THE HEIGHTS WITH GOD, THE HOLY SPIRIT MAKES ITS WAY THROUGH OF ITS OWN ACCORD, WHEREAS THOSE WHO DEVOTE LITTLE TIME TO PRAYER AND COMMUNION WITH GOD HAVE TO ORGANIZE PAINFULLY."
-SADHU SUNDER SINGH

BUT YE, BELOVED, BUILDING UP YOURSELVES ON YOUR MOST
HOLY FAITH, PRAYING IN THE HOLY GHOST.

– Jude 1:20

DATE:

THANKYOU, LORD...

"GROANINGS WHICH CANNOT BE UTTERED ARE OFTEN PRAYERS WHICH CANNOT BE REFUSED."
-C. H. SPURGEON

AND THE SMOKE OF THE INCENSE, WHICH CAME WITH THE
PRAYERS OF THE SAINTS, ASCENDED UP BEFORE GOD OUT OF
THE ANGELS HAND.

— *Revelation 8:4*

DATE:

THANKYOU, LORD...

THE WORD

"GOD'S GREATEST GIFTS TO MAN COME THROUGH TRAVAIL. WHETHER WE LOOK INTO THE SPIRITUAL OR TEMPORAL SPHERE, CAN WE DISCOVER ANYTHING, ANY GREAT REFORM, ANY BENEFICIAL DISCOVERY, ANY SOUL-AWAKENING REVIVAL, WHICH DID NOT COME THROUGH THE TOLLS AND TEARS, THE VIGILS AND BLOOD-SHEDDING OF MEN AND WOMAN WHOSE SUFFERINGS WERE THE PANGS OF ITS BIRTH?"
-F. B. MEYER

LET ALL THOSE THAT SEEK THEE REJOICE AND BE GLAD IN THEE: LET SUCH AS LOVE THY SALVATION SAY CONTINUALLY, THE LORD BE MAGNIFIED.

— Psalms 40:16

DATE:

THE WORD

THANKYOU, LORD...

"SOME PEOPLE BECOME TIRED AT THE END OF TEN MINUTES OR HALF AN HOUR OF PRAYER. WHAT WILL THEY DO WHEN THEY HAVE TO SPEND ETERNITY IN THE PRESENCE OF GOD? WE MUST BEGIN THE HABIT HERE AND BECOME USED TO BEING WITH GOD."
-SADHU SUNDAR SINGH

"COMMIT THY WORKS UNTO THE LORD, AND THY
THOUGHTS SHALL BE ESTABLISHED."
- Proverbs 16:3

AT THE NAME OF *Jesus* E·V·E·R·Y *knee will bow* PHILIPPIANS 2.10

BOWING BEFORE THE THRONE OF GRACE

This kind of praying draws the sweetness out of our relationship with our God. It recognizes Him above all else, and our relation to Him as our Creator and God. As we spend time pouring ourselves before Him in adoration, revelation of His unspeakable grace fills the heart and mind. Our God, like no other, is gracious beyond description. His loving-kindness is better than life itself. His beauty and glory are without comparison! Words fail as we humble ourselves under His mighty hand.

Positional Prayer is simply giving God His rightful place. Several scriptures ascribe to God certain attributes that reveal His position as our Master and Lord. As we open these before Him in adoring worship, it we like an alabaster box of praise, allowing the fragrance of our submission to please His eager nostrils.

SOVEREIGN CREATOR

"God, You are my Creator! You have total Sovereign power of good and evil in my life. I do not know the best way to go, but You do. You see the end from the beginning. Nothing is hidden from Your sight. I give myself completely to Your will. You are the Almighty God and I will trust and follow You." *etc etc [Isaiah 40:8; 43:15; Romans 1:25; 1 Peter 4:19; Revelation 19:6]*

THE POTTER

"Lord, you are the Potter, I am the clay. You can make of me what you will. I cannot change myself. It is only by Your grace and Spirit that I will be changed and formed into the man or woman of God you want me to be. Make me like Jesus. Let the fruits of your Spirit be developed in me. I throw myself upon your mercy, that I would be conformed to the image of Christ." *etc etc [Isaiah 64:8; Jeremiah 18:2-6; Romans 9:21; 2 Timothy 2:21]*

THE VINE

"You are the Vine, Lord, I am the branch. I can do nothing apart from You. All my sufficiency, all my wisdom, every good thing that is in me, is because of You. Only when I am connected to you can I bear fruit. When I am in You, and You are in me, I bear much fruit. Teach me to abide in you, Lord. You supply, I receive. Do not let me act until You supply what is needed." *etc etc [John 15]*

OUR HUSBAND

"I am the wife. You, Lord are the husband. You are the bridegroom, I am the Bride. I love and obey You. I reverence You and honour You. My life and all that I am is covenanted to You. I am Yours and You are mine. We are one. My God, You look after me. You give me security. Your love embraces me. Nothing can separate me from Your love. My only response is to yield and receive, to give myself to You without reservation. I love You." *etc etc [Isaiah 54:5; Romans 7:4; 8:35-39; Hebrews 13:5; Ephesians 5:23-33]*

OUR SHEPHERD

"God, You are my Shepherd. I am the sheep. You lead and I follow. You protect me, nurture me. I follow you. I will not lag behind or try to run ahead. Help me to follow You closely. Take me beside Your still waters. Lead me in paths of righteousness. Lead me to green pastures where I will be satisfied in Your company. God, help me not to struggle, but simply receive from You all that is needed for Your work. Help me to hear Your voice and follow no other." *Etc [Psalm 23; Isaiah 40:11; Matthew 9:36; John 10:11; 1 Peter 2:25]*

There are other scriptures and attributes that God the Holy Spirit will bring to mind as you pray. Allow the incense of adoration to flow from a thankful and humble heart - receiving from the Father the affirmation, security and identity that you need to become whole. Everything we need is found in Him. He is the Source - Let us go and drink from Him!

DATE:

THANKYOU, LORD...

THE WORD

"PRAYER IS REACHING OUT AFTER THE UNSEEN; FASTING IS LETTING GO OF ALL THAT IS SEEN AND TEMPORAL. FASTING HELPS EXPRESS, DEEPEN, CONFIRM THE RESOLUTION THAT WE ARE READY TO SACRIFICE ANYTHING, EVEN OURSELVES TO ATTAIN WHAT WE SEEK FOR THE KINGDOM OF GOD."
-ANDREW MURRAY

I SOUGHT THE LORD, AND HE HEARD ME,
AND DELIVERED ME FROM ALL MY FEARS
- *Psalms 34:4*

DATE:

THANKYOU, LORD...

THE WORD

"CONTINUING INSTANT IN
PRAYER (ROM. 12:12). THE
GREEK IS A METAPHOR TAKEN
FROM HUNTING DOGS THAT
NEVER GIVE OVER THE GAME
TILL THEY HAVE THEIR PREY."
-THOMAS BROOKS

WHEN THOU SAIDST, SEEK YE MY FACE; MY HEART SAID
UNTO THEE, THY FACE, LORD, WILL I SEEK.
— *Psalms 27:8*

DATE:

THANKYOU, LORD...

THE WORD

"IF YOU ARE STRANGERS TO PRAYER YOU ARE STRANGERS TO POWER."
-BILLY SUNDAY

THIS IS THE GENERATION OF THEM THAT SEEK HIM, THAT
SEEK THY FACE, O JACOB. SELAH.

— Psalms 24:6

DATE:

THANKYOU, LORD...

THE WORD

"GIVE YOU YET ANOTHER REASON WHY YOU SHOULD PRAY? I HAVE PREACHED MY VERY HEART OUT. I COULD NOT SAY ANY MORE THAN I HAVE SAID. WILL NOT YOUR PRAYERS ACCOMPLISH THAT WHICH MY PREACHING FAILS TO DO? IS IT NOT LIKELY THAT THE CHURCH HAS BEEN PUTTING FORTH ITS PREACHING HAND BUT NOT ITS PRAYING HAND? OH DEAR FRIENDS! LET US AGONIZE IN PRAYER."
-C. H. SPURGEON

THE LORD LOOKED DOWN FROM HEAVEN UPON THE
CHILDREN OF MEN, TO SEE IF THERE WERE ANY THAT DID
UNDERSTAND, AND SEEK GOD.

— Psalms 14:2

HE HEALS the BROKENHEARTED and BINDS UP their WOUNDS

—Psalm 147.3

DATE:

THANKYOU, LORD...

THE WORD

"PRAYER IS NOT DESIGNED TO
INFORM GOD, BUT TO GIVE
MAN A SIGHT OF HIS MISERY;
TO HUMBLE HIS HEART, TO
EXCITE HIS DESIRE, TO
INFLAME HIS FAITH, TO
ANIMATE HIS HOPE, TO RAISE
HIS SOUL FROM EARTH TO
HEAVEN."
-ADAM CLARKE

THE HUMBLE SHALL SEE THIS, AND BE GLAD; AND YOUR
HEART SHALL LIVE THAT SEEK GOD.

— *Psalms 69:32*

DATE:

THANKYOU, LORD...

THE WORD

"PRAY, O PRAY, MY BROTHER! NEVER, NEVER QUIT YOUR HOLD OF THE FULLNESS OF GOD; FOR TIME IS NEARLY OVER, AND IF THIS FULLNESS BE LOST IT WILL BE LOST FOREVER. I AM ASTONISHED THAT WE DO NOT PRAY MORE, YEA, THAT WE DO NOT LIVE EVERY MOMENT AS ON THE BRINK OF THE ETERNAL WORLD, AND IN THE BLESSED EXPECTATION OF THAT GLORIOUS COUNTRY."
-WILLIAM BRAMWELL

GLORY YE IN HIS HOLY NAME: LET THE HEART OF THEM
REJOICE THAT SEEK THE LORD.

– Psalms 105:3

DATE:

THANKYOU, LORD...

THE WORD

"WORK AS IF EVERYTHING
DEPENDED UPON YOUR
WORK, AND PRAY AS IF
EVERYTHING DEPENDED
UPON YOUR PRAYER."
-WILLIAM BOOTH

BLESSED ARE THEY THAT KEEP HIS TESTIMONIES, AND THAT
SEEK HIM WITH THE WHOLE HEART.
— Psalms 119:2

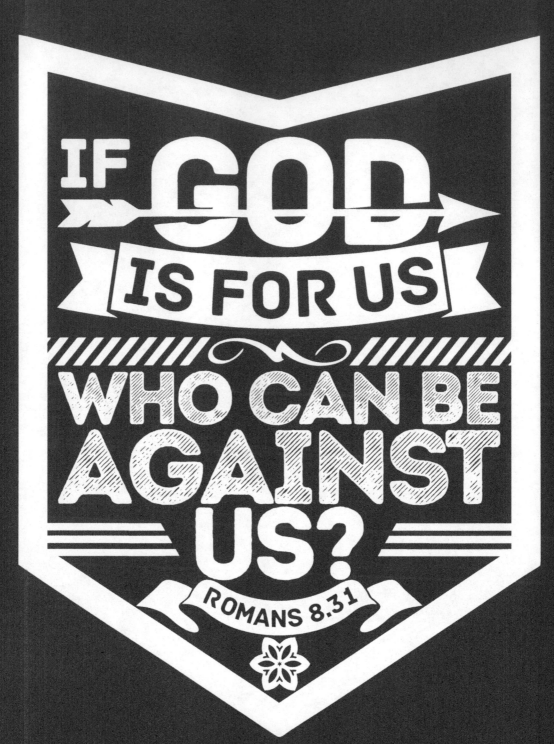

DATE:

THANKYOU, LORD...

THE WORD

"A REAL MINISTER OF THE GOSPEL IS A MAN OF PRAYER. PRAYER IS HIS GRAND EMPLOYMENT, HIS SAFETY, HIS FIRST AND PERPETUAL DUTY; AND UNDER GRACE, THE GRAND SOURCE OF HIS CONSOLATION. OUR INSTRUCTIONS WILL BE ALWAYS BARREN, IF THEY BE NOT WATERED WITH OUR TEARS AND PRAYERS."
-THOMAS COKE

WITH MY WHOLE HEART HAVE I SOUGHT THEE: O LET ME
NOT WANDER FROM THY COMMANDMENTS..

– *Psalms 119:10*

DATE:

THANKYOU, LORD...

THE WORD

> "A MAN MAY STUDY BECAUSE HIS BRAIN IS HUNGRY FOR KNOWLEDGE, EVEN BIBLE KNOWLEDGE. BUT HE PRAYS BECAUSE HIS SOUL IS HUNGRY FOR GOD."
> -LEONARD RAVENHILL

I LOVE THEM THAT LOVE ME; AND THOSE THAT SEEK ME
EARLY SHALL FIND ME.

— Proverbs 7:15

Call TO ME and i will ANSWER you and will tell you Great & Hidden THINGS THAT YOU HAVE NOT KNOWN

Jeremiah 33.3

WANTED: Ferocious Men of Prayer

As men of faith we surely declare that we want to see the will of God in operation. We have prayed more than once, *"Let Your will be done, let Your Kingdom come"*.

Are you ready and willing to become the answer to your own prayer?

God's will is clear, at least on one point:
*"**I will therefore that men pray** every where, lifting up holy hands, without wrath and doubting." (1 Timothy 2:8 KJV)*

There has never been a time when such a call to spiritual arms has been more clear, and indeed more needed.

Manhood has an inherent nature that is ferocious. Savagely fierce and dangerous. Manhood pursues and subdues. It conquers and calls into being.

The devil wants to shackle this Godlike power and do one of two things: tie it to purposes contrary to God and His Kingdom and let it run amok, devastating all that it touches, or conversely, castrate it so we end up with a church full of virtual eunuchs pretending to be 'nice' for a couple of short hours on a Sunday morning before reclaiming their manhood back in the office on Monday.

But the place the Almighty wants this aggressive winning nature to be truly harnessed is in the closet of prayer.

The devil fears nothing more than a man given to prayer.

Fervency is a burning hot passion that spills over into action. No true fire can remain tamed under the grave clothes - it has by its very nature to burst forth and consume. This is the quality of prayer that reaches the nostrils of Heaven!

"The effective, fervent prayer of a righteous man avails much." (James 5:16 NKJV)

Prayer is the voice of the heart. The deep calling unto deep. Men are called not to fill the air with pathetic half-hearted utterances and excuse themselves. No! No! No! Men are called to lend all the might of their being to this one essential work - to labor in the closet of prayer until the very foundations of the world shake with God's power and presence.

Man of God, your search for significance has come to an end. Your seeking for purpose has found its prize. Prayer is your primary pursuit and glorious privilege.

Will you lean in and let Him lead you?

DATE:

THANKYOU, LORD...

THE WORD

"A MINISTER, WHO PRAYS NOT, WHO IS NOT IN LOVE WITH PRAYER, IS NOT A MINISTER OF THE CHURCH OF GOD. HE IS A DRY TREE, WHICH OCCUPIES IN VAIN A PLACE IN CHRIST'S GARDEN. HE IS AN ENEMY, AND NOT A FATHER, OF THE PEOPLE. HE IS A STRANGER, WHO HAS TAKEN THE PLACE OF THE SHEPHERD, AND TO WHOM THE SALVATION OF THE FLOCK IS AN INDIFFERENT THING."
-THOMAS COKE

SEEK YE THE LORD WHILE HE MAY BE FOUND,
CALL YE UPON HIM WHILE HE IS NEAR.
— *Isaiah 55:6*

DATE:

THANKYOU, LORD...

THE WORD

"NO ERUDITION, NO PURITY OF DICTION, NO WIDTH OF MENTAL OUTLOOK, NO FLOWERS OF ELOQUENCE, NO GRACE OF PERSON ATONE FOR LACK OF FIRE. PRAYER ASCENDS BY FIRE. FLAME GIVES PRAYER ACCESS AS WELL AS WINGS, ACCEPTANCE AS WELL AS ENERGY. THERE IS NO INCENSE WITHOUT FIRE; NO PRAYER WITHOUT FLAME."
- E. M. BOUNDS

AND I SET MY FACE UNTO THE LORD GOD, TO SEEK BY
PRAYER AND SUPPLICATIONS, WITH FASTING, AND
SACKCLOTH, AND ASHES.
— Daniel 9:3

PRAISING GOD FOR ANSWERED PRAYER

My Diary of Divine Interventions

My Prayer	Date Prayed	Date Answered

My Prayer	Date Prayed	Date Answered

My Prayer	Date Prayed	Date Answered

My Prayer	Date Prayed	Date Answered

"THE EFFECTUAL FERVENT PRAYER OF
A RIGHTEOUS WOMAN AVAILETH MUCH."
JAMES 5:16

My Prayer	Date Prayed	Date Answered

My Prayer	Date Prayed	Date Answered

My Prayer	Date Prayed	Date Answered

My Prayer	Date Prayed	Date Answered

My Prayer	Date Prayed	Date Answered

"NOW UNTO HIM THAT IS ABLE TO DO EXCEEDING ABUNDANTLY ABOVE ALL
THAT WE ASK OR THINK, ACCORDING TO THE POWER THAT WORKETH IN US,
UNTO HIM *BE* GLORY IN THE CHURCH BY CHRIST JESUS THROUGHOUT ALL
AGES, WORLD WITHOUT END. AMEN." EPHESIANS 3:20–21

My Prayer	Date Prayed	Date Answered

My Prayer	Date Prayed	Date Answered

My Prayer	Date Prayed	Date Answered

My Prayer	Date Prayed	Date Answered

My Prayer	Date Prayed	Date Answered

"VERILY GOD HATH HEARD ME; HE HATH
ATTENDED TO THE VOICE OF MY PRAYER."
PSALMS 66:19

My Prayer	Date Prayed	Date Answered

My Prayer	Date Prayed	Date Answered

My Prayer	Date Prayed	Date Answered

My Prayer	Date Prayed	Date Answered

My Prayer	Date Prayed	Date Answered

"I WILL PRAISE THEE: FOR THOU HAST HEARD ME,
AND ART BECOME MY SALVATION."
PSALMS 118:21

IT IS
finished

JOHN 19:30

About The Authors

David, Larna and their family are passionately following Jesus and seeking every day and in every way to build His Kingdom.

As ordained pastors and ministers they long to see a fresh move of God's Holy Spirit, and feel privileged to play a small part in encouraging you to continue seeking God with fervency.

Blessings from our household to yours,

David & Larna

DON'T FORGET TO PICK UP YOUR WEAPONS...

Access to the Spirit Life Bible School
JesusChrist.co.uk

Tabernacle Prayer
Interactive Guide
and Video Workshop
JesusChrist.co.uk/tabernacle-prayer

Made in the USA
Coppell, TX
12 February 2023

12671779R00122